PAPER TRAILS

A HISTORY OF
BRITISH COLUMBIA
AND
YUKON
COMMUNITY NEWSPAPERS

Paper Trails: A history of British Columbia and Yukon Community Newspapers.

All Rights Reserved.

Published by Arch Communications / BCYCNA

Copyright 1999 by George Allan Affleck

For more information contact:
BCYCNA
230-1380 Burrard Street
Vancouver, BC, V6Z 2B7
Tel: 604-669-9222
Fax: 604-684-4713
archbooks@canada.com
info@bccommunitynews.com

CANADIAN CATLOGUING IN PUBLICATION DATA
Affleck, George Allan, 1964-
    A history of BC and Yukon community newspapers

Includes index.
ISBN 0-9684322-0-4

    1. Community newspapers—British Columbia—History.
2. Community newspapers—Yukon Territory—History. 3. Community
newspapers—British Columbia—History—Anecdotes. 4. Community
newspapers—Yukon Territory—Histroy—Anecdotes. 1. Title.
PN4914.C63A34 1999   071'.11   C99-900324-0

Cover Design: Sarah Brown
Cover Photo: Carson Avenue, Quesnel, 1912. Quesnel & District Museum
    1991901 AD 172.17
Page Design and Layout: Patty Osborne, Vancouver Desktop

Printed and bound in Canada.

To Pernilla

TABLE OF CONTENTS

PREFACE

Newspapers, as the myth goes, are a licence to print money. But few publishers — with the exception, perhaps, of Joseph Coyle — would agree. Coyle, you see, was an enterprising publisher who came pretty close to actually running money off on his press. The founder of the *Smithers Interior News* was also the owner of the only paper cutter in town in the early 1900s. And he earned extra revenue by cutting sheets of freshly printed currency for the local bank.

That's one of the many entertaining stories you'll find in this book about the early days of the community newspaper industry in British Columbia. There were plenty of colourful characters about in those days, which leads you to wonder what has happened since. Those of us in the industry today seem rather pale by comparison. However, perhaps history will one day put us in a different, more colourful light.

This book does not attempt to chronicle every single community newspaper that has been published in B.C. and the Yukon. Such a task would be formidable, if not impossible. Instead, it has relied on the 100 plus member newspapers of the B.C. & Yukon Community Newspapers Association (BCYCNA) along with a several others to supply the historical information about their newspapers and other, earlier papers in their communities. For their assistance, we are very grateful. We must also credit the efforts of the late Irving Wilson and his wife Frances who 25 years ago published the first history of BCYCNA members, and whose work we have incorporated here. We would also like to thank George Affleck for all the work he has put into this project. When the book was proposed, the association had a somewhat fuzzy vision of what it might be. George was quick to develop that vision into something more focused.

We hope you enjoy the book.

—Penny Graham, President, BCYCNA & Publisher,
The Squamish Chief
—Tony Richards, Chairman, BCYCNA History Book
Committee & Publisher, *Gulf Islands Driftwood*

WHEN WE WERE WEEKLIES

They were called weeklies in those days, in the 1960s, and while there was little about them that was glamorous, they sure were fun.

One year in Salmon Arm made me forget the 15 years I spent at the Vancouver dailies, which was about as much fun as a root canal.

Dennis Marshall was publisher of the *Salmon Arm Observer*. He had a devilish look in his eyes the morning he returned from coffee with his cronies.

"Gonna run colour this week," says Marshall.

"Colour? Impossible. That old, flatbed press doesn't do colour."

"Watch me."

We not only watched, we were soon doing colour ourselves by squeezing a spray bomb to add a touch of green to an ad as the press rumbled back and forth on its bed.

This after only a couple of months away from the new, million-dollar showcase Pacific Press building in Vancouver?

Perfect.

The Hacker brothers, Arvid Lundell, Clare Rivers, Frank Richards, John and Alexis MacNaughton, the Dunnings, George Coupeland, Stan McKinnon, Frances and Irving Wilson, these were some of the publishers who carried on the work of B.C. Weekly Newspaper Association pioneers by gathering at the Hotel Vancouver each year as the leaves turned golden.

The 1937 BC & Yukon Weekly Newspapers Association Convention.

Canadian Weekly Newspapers Annual Convention.

Most of them knew how to party, all of them knew how to talk about newspapers. More than one piano was found the next morning in the lobby of the hotel or when meetings moved to Richmond, at pool side.

Good times, good people.

There was, in 1967, a nut living somewhere on the coast who had forecast that Vancouver Island was about to disappear into the sea as the result of a horrific earthquake.

In response, the *Campbell River Upper-Islander* produced an earthquake edition — two pages of spoof, highlighted by a slash of heavy-border tape that looked like a crack as it zigzagged across the pages.

You could do those kinds of things because offset was becoming part of the industry. Besides, everyone was having fun.

In Prince George work crews had not attended to frost boils like they should have that spring. *The Progress* used a Volkswagen Dinky-Toy perched on the edge of a hole in the road and photographed up close. The result was a page one picture showing a vehicle disappearing into a crater. It was the talk of the town. It also got action from city fathers.

In Port Alberni an unsuspecting alderman, mad at news coverage of council, called the *Times* pink in his nearly-illiterate letter to the editor. He should not have done that for the next paper had a pink wash across the front page and a headline that explained: "We're pink — for today only." His unedited letter was there too.

No doubt about it, we were having fun.

The *Ladysmith-Chemainus Chronicle* was founded in 1908 by David Mark Carley, one of the old-time "boomers" (tramp printers who went from newspaper to newspaper in the old days to work either in the shop or the newsroom). The paper has gone through its fair share of owners over the years, all with great stories to tell. But Christmas 1974 is a particularly memorable time.

It was especially snowy on the island that season, but there was no snow in the Ladysmith area. By comparison, there was a foot in Campbell River and varying amounts of snow in between.

Returning to work from a week off and faced with little news other than the fact that there was snow everywhere else on the island, the *Chronicle* staff decided to have some fun with the weather.

They ran a picture of a yellow banana across the top half of page one and proclaimed Ladysmith to be the banana belt of B.C. A collage of beach photos taken the summer before supported the banana.

Prior to press time, the weatherman promised there would be no more snow anywhere on the island.

So, roll the presses!

The next morning, the *Chronicle* was late being distributed to downtown stores because there was snow in the streets. Ten inches of it.

To this day shop owners will tell you that they don't shovel snow in Ladysmith, they shovel bananas.

As the years slipped by, the weeklies became more sophisticated. They changed their name to the community press and group publishing became commonplace as the newspapers had known in the 50s and 60s.

The good, old days? You bet.

Because in what other industry could you have had so much fun and be paid while doing it?   —*Rollie Rose*

Vancouver Island / Midcoast

Monday
MAGAZINE

COWICHAN VALLEY'S COMMUNITY NEWSPAPER
SUNDAY CITIZEN

NORTH
ISLAND
GAZETTE

The Parksville / Qualicum Beach
Morning Sun

The Powell River
PEAK

The Pictorial

Gulf Islands
Driftwood

BELLA COOLA, COAST MOUNTAIN NEWS

Angela Hall's plan was to retire. She and her husband packed up all their belongings and moved to Bella Coola from Vancouver in the mid-1980s. But Hall could not stand to do nothing. So she landed a job at the local newspaper.

The *Coast Mountain Courier* was founded on November 7, 1984 and was the brainchild of Dan Dunaway and his friend Peter Hess. Bella Coola had seen many newspapers come and go over the years, starting with a little newsletter called the *Advertiser*, which began publication in the 1930s. But none seemed to survive until the *Courier* came along.

In 1989 Dunaway, now the sole owner, had had enough of the newspaper industry. Fascinated with the business after having worked in the office for a few years, Hall decided to buy the paper from Dunaway.

"It was a hard row to hoe at first," she says. "I didn't have any newspaper experience except for what I had helped Dan with."

But with a solid background as a writer and an office administrator, Hall thought she was up for the challenge.

The first thing she did was update the office equipment, buying four new computers, a scanner, a fax and some darkroom supplies.

"Then we changed the name of the newspaper from *Coast Mountain Courier* to the *Coast Mountain News* because we kept getting calls for courier service," says Hall.

The paper has prospered under Hall's guidance.

"It's granny owned and operated," she says. "And I love it."

CAMPBELL RIVER COURIER-ISLANDER

Thomson Newspapers purchased the *Campbell River Courier-Islander* newspaper in the 1980s. Since that time the *Courier-Islander* has undergone many changes, including launching the *North Islander*, a free-distribution weekend paper that covers the northern half of Vancouver Island.

3

The newspaper celebrated its 50th anniversary in 1995, one year before Campbell River municipality celebrated its 50th anniversary of incorporation.

The *Courier-Islander* endured a difficult time when its sister paper, the *Comox District Free Press*, was closed in the early 90s after a lengthy labour dispute.

That left the *Courier-Islander* without its press site. But an aggressive emergency plan utilizing printing plants in Port Alberni, Victoria and Vancouver enabled the *Courier-Islander* to survive near disaster.

In 1998 *Courier-Islander* publisher and former editor Neil Cameron named 26-year-old Shari Cummins as the first female editor of the paper in its 50-year history.

As it has throughout the years, the *Courier-Islander* continues to bring home numerous awards for its achievements in editorial, photo work and special publications.

—*Neil Cameron*

CAMPBELL RIVER MIRROR

The *Campbell River Mirror* was founded in 1970 by a consortium of local businessmen concerned that the other two papers in town, which had recently come under the same ownership, would have a monopoly. It was purchased by Gerry and Vera Soroka. Under the Sorokas, the *Mirror* experienced a period of expansion. In 1993, the Sorokas sold the paper to David Black's Island Publishers Ltd. In 1994, it expanded to publishing twice weekly with a *Weekender* publication, then to a Wednesday and Friday *Mirror* after the *Weekender* was spun off in 1995. It became a separate regional weekly covering the North Island from Fanny Bay to Port Hardy. One other major change came in 1996 when the *Mirror* converted from a combined paid and free subscription publication to a Total Market Coverage product delivered free to 14,500 households in Campbell River. In 1997, the *Mirror* was judged, for the second year in a row, the best newspaper in Canada in its circulation class by the Canadian Community Newspapers Association.

COLWOOD/GOLDSTREAM
NEWS GAZETTE

They mortgaged a Dutch cutter to launch a newspaper. Two decades later, its founders have no idea what became of that sailboat, but their newspaper is still sailing along. The first edition of the *Goldstream Gazette* was published March 17, 1976 and delivered to 8,500 homes and businesses in the Western Communities of Greater Victoria.

Its birth was part accident-part luck, involving a sudden change of plans and a lot of hard labour. At least that's the story that emerges from the paper's three founders — George Manning, Verne Percival and Mike Crossman.

Oh, and let's not forget the sailboat.

Crossman bought the boat in England in 1974 and then took it on an 18-month voyage through the Caribbean, the Panama Canal and the Hawaiian Islands before returning to Vancouver Island in 1975. Shortly after his return, Crossman hooked up with Manning and Percival. Their plan was to purchase the *Juan de Fuca News*, a weekly which had served the Western Communities since the late 1950s. When the *News* deal collapsed, Percival and Manning figured they'd start their own newspaper. There was just one problem: they hardly had any money. But one of them had this 33-foot sailboat.

"I think it was just a logical idea," Crossman says. "It was a matter of, 'How are we going to come up with some money? Hey, wait a minute, there's a boat.'"

All three also had something else of value: newspaper experience. Crossman had worked for years as a news photographer at daily newspapers in Ontario. He and Manning had met in the early 1970s in Sidney, where Manning was editor of the *Review* and where Crossman ran a photo studio and did darkroom work and photography for the paper.

Manning and Percival went back even further to when Manning was publications director for the *Martlet*, the University of Victoria's student newspaper. Percival was production manager at the *Juan de Fuca News*, which produced the *Martlet*.

Later, at the *Review*, Manning got to know Percival even better, as the *News* also did the *Review's* composing.

Bob Bierman, 1998

"We came out here to buy the *Juan de Fuca News*," Manning says. "That was the plan. In November 1975 we took over management of the *Juan de Fuca News* and we were working through the process of buying it. But the deal kept changing. And finally in January 1976, some time in late January, it was clear, it wasn't going to happen."

He recalls discussing the situation with Crossman and concluding that they had just spent three months learning the Western Communities and its market.

As for Percival, he had grown up in the Western Communities. And he had worked at the *News* since the early 1960s when he was in high school. So they decided to start their own paper, using Crossman's sailboat as collateral.

"Very shortly after we financed this thing, we realized the actual market value (of the sailboat) was quite a bit less than the appraisal," Manning says. "And quite a bit less than the loan. So we couldn't afford to sell it because we wouldn't be able to pay off the loan. So we had to keep varnishing the thing."

Crossman confirms that the replacement value of the vessel, built

6

in 1931 of very fine teak, was much higher than its market value. "We finally dropped the price and sold the sailboat when we could afford to pay off the loan," says Crossman.

In the last 20 years, the *Gazette* has undergone some building and rebuilding too. The name changed in 1993 — to the *News Gazette* — to reflect its membership in Greater Victoria's News Group weeklies. The News Group is part of Island Publishers, of which the *Gazette* became a cornerstone in 1984. "In the best sense of the word, we were opportunistic entrepreneurs," Manning says of the company's birth and success. Or as Percival put it: "We did things by the seat of our pants." For example, much of the start-up took place in the Westwind Hotel coffee shop, where they interviewed prospective staff and received telephone messages.

In 1981, the *Goldstream Gazette* bought its own press. Manning says seeing their paper roll off their own press in 1981 was just as special as watching the first edition being born. The printer who had printed the *Gazette* up to that point didn't think so, though. When Manning, as a matter of courtesy, informed him in 1980 that he'd be getting his own press, the printer immediately refused to print the paper any longer.

So Manning arranged to have the paper printed in Williams Lake, until the *Gazette* got its own press. That went on for about year. And despite the distances and occasional bad weather, the *Gazette* never missed a mail deadline.

The first press consisted of four units of a 1960s vintage Rockwell-Goss Community Press. But these weren't just any four units. They had serial numbers 1, 3, 4, and 5.

Island Publishers, which was the 14th owner of the press, traded in unit #1 back to the manufacturer for a newer model a few years ago. The press has been rebuilt and is often displayed at newspaper conventions. The purchase of the press also brought community newspaper magnate David Black into the picture. Manning et al had purchased the press from Black's Cariboo Press. As part of the deal, Black became a minority shareholder in the *Gazette*. Black is now the primary shareholder of the *Gazette*, and about 80 other publications on Vancouver Island, in the B.C. Interior, Alberta and the Puget Sound area of Washington state. Shortly after Black got involved with the *Gazette*, the business underwent a transformation.

Photo by Gerry Fairbrother, Comox Valley Echo

"We convinced him to buy the Sidney paper, which he did," Manning says. Then he bought the Ladysmith paper and printing plant from well-known newspaperman Rollie Rose.

Island Publishers was born and Manning was made general manager. And he oversaw the acquisition of another dozen Island weeklies, plus several specialty publications. The chain continues to grow and produce some of Canada's most respected journalists. Humble beginnings, a used sailboat, and a little bit of luck sure can lead to amazing things.

TOTEM TIMES — CANADIAN FORCES BASE, COMOX

The first *CFB Comox Totem Times* was published on March 17, 1960, which makes it the oldest newspaper in the Comox Valley. It inherited this claim to fame after the untimely demise of the *Comox District Free Press*. (They were twice as old and closed down after a lengthy labour dispute a few years ago.)

The *Totem Times*, a military base newspaper, is currently a biweekly tabloid although it was, at one time, a weekly broadsheet. It has acquired, over time, a decent reputation among base papers and contributes in its way to our Canadian air force heritage.

During the years that the paper was run by a volunteer staff, it won the Canadian Community Newspapers Association's Best Military Newspaper Award six times between 1981 and 1992.

The *Totem Times* has been produced and managed by a succession of serving and retired military people over the years, with the help of few employees and many volunteers.

The *Times* is currently replacing an outdated computer and good old-fashioned cut and paste with modern equipment that will bring the publication up to the 1990s standards — just in time for the 21st century!

—*Master Corporal Edith Cuerrier*

COMOX VALLEY ECHO

One of the few independent, locally owned broadsheets in Canada, the *Comox Valley Echo* is a community newspaper formed in late 1994.

The *Echo* is something of a "phoenix" rising from the ashes of the long-running *Comox District Free Press*, which closed in 1994 after 103 years of continuous publication under several names.

Many of the principals behind the *Echo* venture were involved with the *Free Press*, including founding publisher Dave MacDonald, editor Debra Martin and business manager Virginia Hughes.

Their many years of publishing experience quickly established the *Echo* as a respected member of the newspaper community. Using high-end Macintosh publishing technology and employing a skilled production, advertising and editorial staff, the paper has distinguished itself for vibrant editorial and advertising design from its outset.

Begun as a weekly on Dec. 9, 1994, the *Echo* successfully moved to twice-weekly publication in September 1995, and prints a colour-front broadsheet and frequent supplements every Tuesday and Friday. Distributed to 19,000 homes in the Comox Valley and winner of numerous awards.

Another hallmark of the paper is its dedication to community sponsorships. The *Echo* was founding sponsor of the local Buskers' Faire, created the Hole-In-One contest for the United Way, is involved with the Wine Festival in support of the local college's library foundation, helps out with the Salvation army grocery drive each Christmas, and participates in many other charitable causes.

"Getting a new paper started has been a real challenge in this day and age," says publisher Dave MacDonald. "But our goal is to truly represent this community."

The *Echo's* staff looks forward to carrying on a positive relationship with the Comox Valley for many years to come.

COURTENAY COMOX VALLEY RECORD

The *Comox Valley Record* is history in the making. A relative newcomer to the Fourth Estate, the *Record's* first issue hit the street on March 26, 1986. It represented a bold venture by David Black's Island Publishers Ltd. into a market long dominated by the *Comox District Free Press*. Reg Cowie was the first publisher and Lon Wood (now a columnist with the *Victoria Times-Colonist*) sat at the editor's desk. They guided the fortunes of a weekly broadsheet that quickly established a solid base of readership and advertising. This with a small staff and limited facilities.

The early success prompted an increased publication frequency in 1989 as the *Comox Valley Record* became a twice-weekly. At the same time, a switch to tabloid format made it easier to read and a more distinct entity on local newsstands.

In its formative years, the *Record* was written in Courtenay, with the editor and advertising manager then travelling to Duncan to have the issue typeset and pasted up. As the newspaper grew, all in-house advertising, editorial and page production was done in Courtenay.

The *Comox Valley Record* has had three downtown Courtenay locations, each increasingly larger to accommodate staff growth and technological updates. The Record celebrated its 12th anniversary in 1998 by moving into its own modern office building at 765 McPhee Avenue in Courtenay.

Jim Odo, Courtenay Comox Free Press, *1977*.

The move has allowed the paper to continue to grow and expand to keep pace with population growth in the Comox Valley. The current circulation is 20,300 and growing. The readership area ranges from Oyster River in the north to Fanny Bay in the South and includes Denman and Hornby Islands.

To provide informative and comprehensive coverage to such a wide area, the *Record* employs 35 staff members plus contract distribution drivers and a dedicated newspaper carrier force of 233.

Guiding the fortunes of the *Comox Valley Record* are publisher Grant Lawrence and editor Bruce Winfield. Lawrence follows in the footsteps of Jim Odo, Jay Luchsinger and Murray Francis, who held the post after Cowie. Winfield has worn the editor's cap for the past eight years after taking over from David Marsden, who replaced Wood.

Over the years, the *Comox Valley Record* has been the recipient of several B.C. & Yukon Community Newspapers Association and Canadian Community Newspapers Association awards. The list of accomplishments include the CCNA's prestigious Best All Round honors in 1996.

Although just 12 years young, the *Comox Valley Record* has firmly established itself as a major force in a growing market.

DUNCAN CITIZEN

It's been a wild ride at the *Citizen* in Duncan. The *Citizen's* short history has been coloured by aggressive optimism. When everyone said Duncan was too small to support two newspapers and a shopper, Vancouver Island publisher E.W. Bickle put his hand in his deep pockets and said he could make it happen. That was 1985. More than a decade later, the paper is still making it happen, challenging Duncan's other paper and making big noise in a little city.

Phil Bickle ran his newspaper publishing empire from Courtenay. He took it on as a personal challenge to start up the *Citizen*. It was only months after the *Cowichan News* and the 80-year-old *Cowichan Leader* merged into the *Cowichan News Leader*, leaving Duncan with one paper and a successful shopper, the *Pictorial*.

Common wisdom said a city where the two-paper balance had already failed would never support two papers again. Bickle armed himself with process colour, a lean staff of seven and a commitment to show the community the brighter side of their news. The *Citizen* hit the streets on December 12, 1985.

The war stories are great. Scoops, winning over clients, losing clients again only to woo them back. More scoops. But Bickle had a secret weapon in the person of Andy Bigg, his publishing consultant. Bigg was the one-time owner of the competition, the originator of the *Pictorial* and a 70-year-old veteran of the newspaper business. He knew his stuff.

The first issues were put out with next-to-no equipment. Dave Rubenstein, the original sports editor (read one half of the leanest editorial staff), now in sales, wrote all his stories on a 1950s manual typewriter — the letter K always stuck.

Those who were on staff back then tell stories of practical jokes, some dreamed up, some acted out. One included the portable office half the staff occupied. It seems the other half who were not in there

Bill Lam (Richmond Times), Manfred Tempelmayr (Duncan Pictorial),
Premier Van der Zalm.

often thought of locking the place up from the outside. It never happened and to this day the sales staff have no idea how close they were to being locked in that stifling hot portable after the umpteenth copy change on an ad.

Deadlines were followed by midnight runs to the press, with the near-hysteria that follows too many hours of work.

"We used to think the *News Leader* was following us," says Dianne Gordon from the production department. "We'd have to take the flats out to our car really late to take it to be printed and we always had the feeling someone from the other paper was going to bonk us over the head and grab the paper."

No one was ever bonked, and no one ever stole the flats; but the battle has not been without victories, not without casualties.

"Sometimes we've been our own worst enemy," says Rubenstein.

The *Best Of* is something the long-timers still groan about. A turning point that the paper has struggled to leave behind ever since.

The *Best Of* was an advertising promotion. The sales staff sold *Best Of* spots to one business in every category imaginable, alienating a long list of *Not* the *Best Of* clients.

The paper was hurt — readership and advertising revenue declined.

Bickle had already sold his interest in the paper to Netmar, the company that distributed the paper (using a proudly boasted "computer-controlled system.") in the late 1980s. Netmar moved the Thursday edition to Sunday. The Wednesday edition was added shortly after. In 1990 Thomson Canada Ltd. bought out the chain of papers. And in 1998 the paper has turned another corner. Hollinger has taken ownership. Editor Tony Kant (editor #4) and publisher Warren Nerby are at the helm, pushing the 12-member staff through the paces of meeting two tight deadlines, winning (and winning back) customers and giving the community an alternative view of the news in their community. It's business as usual.

DUNCAN NEWS LEADER

Since the April 28, 1905 publication of the first four-page, 8.5" BY 11" *Cowichan Leader*, the publication has undergone several transformations, and has grown steadily.

Today's publication is vastly different from the original *Leader*. It serves an entirely different community with different issues and concerns.

Mass media didn't exist at the turn of the century, says publisher Manfred Tempelmayr. Local newspapers were the only means to access information.

"There wasn't mass media as we know it," he says. "Even radios would have been rare."

People now turn on the six o'clock news for their regional and international news. The only way for newspapers to thrive is to offer something TV cannot: strong local coverage.

"We don't exist if we don't give the community what it wants," says Tempelmayr. "There's nothing in the paper that's not relevant to the community."

In 90-plus years of writing community news the paper has undergone several shifts in direction. In the half-century after its 1905 start, the *Leader* changed hands a few times, finally ending up under

Northwest Publications Limited, and grew to seven columns and 12 pages.

In 1966 the *Pictorial*, then a separate paper, came into being. It was owned by Andy Bigg, an experienced publisher. A free-circulating tabloid, this paper was soon popular.

In 1971 Bigg bought the competing *Leader*.

The dealings weren't done yet. In 1976, the *Cowichan News* got a start. This broadsheet was sold to Tempelmayr in 1978, who sold it to David Black in 1984. Tempelmayr has remained at the helm since.

Later in 1984, Black also bought the *Leader* and the *Pictorial*, merging the three. Since then, the *Cowichan News Leader* has come out every Wednesday, the *Pictorial* every Saturday.

With changing times comes changing pressures. The 1905 papers relied mainly on subscription payments. Because of competition, the current paper is free, relying almost solely on advertising revenue.

In 1975 the *Leader*, then separate from the *Pictorial*, had a circulation of 10,000 with a subscription costing $15 a year, for a total of $150,000. In today's dollars, that would be an equivalent to about $400,000 in revenue.

This shortfall means the paper doesn't have as many reporters as Tempelmayr would like, who says a reporter can spend two or three hours on a long-term issue such as water shortages or waste disposal when two or three days would not exhaust it. But that two or three hours is more than any regional newspaper or television news broadcast can spend on North Cowichan and Duncan issues. And that makes staff at the *Duncan News Leader* proud.

ESQUIMALT NEWS

The *Esquimalt News* is the most recent in a long line of incarnations of community newspapers that have hit the streets on Wednesdays.

According to Esquimalt municipal archives, the *Esquimalt Leader* was the first community newspaper in Esquimalt. D. H. "Bert" Nelson served as both publisher and editor of the newspaper from the time it hit the stands on Wednesday, October 10, 1962 to the time it was renamed the *Esquimalt Sentinel* on November 4, 1964. At that time Peter R. Gardner took over the helm as both editor and publisher. Both the *Leader* and *Sentinel* were published by the Leader Publishing Company Ltd.

On January 22, 1975, a new newspaper appeared on the scene, the *Esquimalt Sun*. It was headed up by Dan Heffernan and manager James Borsman.

About the same time, the *Esquimalt Advertiser* was launched. It was published every Wednesday, starting November 10, 1976. Frank Hird-Rutter was publisher and Derek Rhind was editor.

On November 11, 1981, the *Esquimalt Star* hit the streets. The publisher continued to be Dan Heffernan, who also had been the publisher of the *Esquimalt Sun*.

Editor Floyd Cowan eventually took over as publisher May 8, 1985 where he remained until the newspaper was purchased by Island Publishers and renamed the *Esquimalt News*.

The first edition of the *Esquimalt News* was published January 4, 1989.

General manager was Steve Hanson. The newspaper's first editor was Jackie Pleasants.

Since its inception, there have been different publishers and editors at the *Esquimalt News*. Current publisher Rick Passmore has been at the helm since 1997. Current editor Alanna Jorde was hired on as a reporter in 1994 and took over as editor a year later.

The *Esquimalt News* is part of Island Publishers Victoria News Group that also includes sister community newspapers *Goldstream News Gazette*, *Oak Bay News*, *Peninsula News Review*, *Saanich News*, *Sooke News* and *Victoria News*. In the spring of 1995, the News Group launched a second edition of its community newspapers called the *Weekend Edition*.

GOLD RIVER RECORD

The Village of Gold River is an "instant village" established by the province of British Columbia in 1965 in conjunction with a pulp mill that was being built by the Tahsis Company. The first recorded newspaper in the village was *Between the Gold and the Heber* started by

Photo by Derrick Lundy, Gulf Islands Driftwood

Joan McKay in early 1968. This was succeeded in 1970 by the *Record*, published by Bert and Joan Donovan on 14-inch foolscap. During a brief interlude in 1974 the *Record* stopped publishing and the *Gold River Nugget*, published by Ray Olson, took its place. This did not last long and the Donovans resumed publishing the *Record*.

In 1978 the paper changed to a tab format, then in 1982 it changed again to a broadsheet. It was being published bi-weekly when it was sold to Miriam Trevis in April of 1986. The name was changed to the *Nootka News*, and for a while it was published weekly.

In May of 1987 the paper was purchased by Leslie and Gerry Hunter, the name was changed back to the *Record* and it was published bi-weekly with a print run of about 1,200.

In August of 1995 the Hunters sold the paper to Lynne and Jerry West, the current publishers, who changed the format back to tab. Currently the paper is a bi-weekly with a press run of 1,800 and primarily serves the communities of Gold River, Tahsis, Zeballos and

Kyuquot. There is also distribution in Port Alice, Port McNeill, Woss and Campbell River as well as mail subscriptions throughout B.C.

GULF ISLANDS DRIFTWOOD

Tony Richards considers himself lucky. A lot of kids cringe at the thought of inheriting the family business, but Richards loves his job as publisher and managing editor of the *Gulf Islands Driftwood*.

"This is a really neat business to be in, " Richards admits. "Where else can you work in sales, manufacturing, distribution and editorial all in the same day."

Richards and his wife Alice inherited the newspaper, located in Ganges on Salt Spring Island, from his parents, who bought it in 1967 from Jim and Arlene Ward. They had purchased the *Driftwood* a few years before from Woody Fisher, who launched the paper in 1960. It was the Wards who changed the name from the *Salt Spring Island Driftwood* to the *Gulf Islands Driftwood*.

When Frank and Barbara Richards bought the paper and moved their family from Sidney, B.C., they may have not realized they were creating a mini-dynasty.

But from day one the whole family was involved in every aspect of the paper's production.

"We did everything from addressing papers to writing stories," says Tony Richards, who was 16 when they moved to Ganges.

Today, it is still a family business. Alice is production manager, son

(l to r) Alan Black, Lynn Lashbrook, Frank Richards, Steven Dills, 1978.

Robin is a typesetter and Frank Richards continues to write a weekly column.

Not surprisingly, the family has seen a great deal of change over the years. Not only has the independently owned newspaper tripled in size, it has become a more serious journalistic publication.

"We are less chatty and less informal now," Richard says. "We don't do as much social or gossip news anymore."

The fact that more people live on the Islands makes it easier to find hard news and gives you more potential for profit. But the Gulf Islands are like a small town; when you write something that a person believes to be incorrect or unbalanced, you are made aware of it.

"It keeps us honest knowing we are so close to the readership," says Richards.

He believes keeping in touch with an ever-changing readership is also the key to the *Driftwood's* success.

"Trying to satisfy such a wide range of people with such diverse backgrounds is a real challenge," he says. But judging by the newspaper's success, Tony Richards and clan are on to something.

LADYSMITH-CHEMAINUS CHRONICLE

The *Ladysmith-Chemainus Chronicle* was established by David Mark Carley as competition to the *Ladysmith Standard* and rolled off the presses on March 10, 1908.

Assisted by his wife, Mary, Carley settled into this booming young coal port, and guided its paper of record through those early years.

Ladysmith – just four years older than its newspaper – was founded because of coal magnate James Dunsmuir's dissatisfaction with the shipping situation in Nanaimo.

In its early days, it was a rowdy town marked by a startling 17 pubs, and a disastrous mine explosion that killed 12 men, and sparked some of the most vicious strikes in B.C.'s history.

Carley sold out to Tom Collinge in 1921, and retired to Victoria. But his example of sticking with the *Chronicle* was followed by each of his successors. In its 90 years of existence, the paper has only had six owners, none of whom held it for less than a decade.

Collinge, the former manager of a Port Alberni weekly, saw the paper through the passing of one chapter of Ladysmith's history, and the birth of another.

The mine closed in 1931. Combined with the onset of the Depression, this turned a once-bustling community of 4,000 into a shadow of what it was.

But in 1935, Mother Nature turned things around.

A massive storm knocked down a huge stand of timber near the town, and the Comox Logging Company moved in to reap the profits. They stayed on, and provided a steady job source that kept Ladysmith stable for several years. Forestry has continued to be the mainstay of the community for most of the rest of the century.

Collinge held onto the *Chronicle* until 1942, when he sold out to Robert Hindmarch Jr., A.W. Hindmarch, and S.A. Hindmarch – brothers from Nanaimo.

It was during the Hindmarch period that he paper expanded its scope from Ladysmith to the neighbouring community of Chemainus, seven kilometres to the south.

The brothers started the *Chemainus Herald*, in 1943, which was managed out of a separate office in Chemainus, but printed in the Ladysmith plant.

Chemainus was older than Ladysmith, a company town, built around a history of sawmills, the first of which was built in about 1860. Since then, the Victoria Lumber Company, and MacMillan Bloedel have operated a succession of mills on the shores of the town's harbor, fed by timber from the Island's rich forests.

In 1953, Island Publishers, a company formed by John McNaughton, purchased the papers, then associate editor of the *Brandon Daily Sun*.

After 10 years as publisher and editor of both papers, McNaughton decided to combine the two into one, and first published it as the *Ladysmith-Chemainus Chronicle* in 1963.

Operating out of the same small "character" office on High Street as his predecessors, McNaughton – known for his integrity – became a pillar of the community for 20 years.

But illness eventually forced him to devote less time to the *Chronicle* than he would have liked.

He eventually sold out in 1974 to Rollie Rose, a veteran newsman

Left to right: R.P. Maclean, Kelowna; Lou Griffith, Quesnel; Frank Harris, Vernon; Arvid Lundell, Revelstoke; Les Barlieu, Chilliwack; Cecil Hacker, Abbotsford; Edgar Dunning, Ladner; Lang Sands, Abbotsford.

who had most recently been publisher of the *Port Alberni Valley Times*.

When Rose took over, the *Chronicle* had just one staffer, and was producing only eight pages a week. One critic told him he would have to turn it into a shopper to feed his family.

He didn't.

Bolstered by a late seventies growth spurt in what had been a dormant Ladysmith economy, Rose bought his own press in 1979, and changed the direction of Island Publishing.

By the early '80s, he was printing 14 papers, and all the Island's Safeway flyers, out of his new shop on High Street. He said his high point came in 1982, when the paper was named best in its class in all of Canada.

But with the independents on the Island starting to get swallowed up in the 1980s, Rose decided his pockets were not deep enough to fight it out. The *Chronicle* (and, more importantly, its press) joined the ranks of chain ownership in 1984, when Rose sold to David Black, who, he said, simply made him an offer he couldn't refuse.

Black's first move was to install Manfred Tempelmayr as publisher.

It was during this period, in 1990, when the *Chronicle* abandoned its long-time broadsheet format, and switched to the more popular tab size.

Two years later, forced out by the space demands of a rapidly growing press operation, the newspaper office was on the move again, this time to 341 Front Avenue.

As Tempelmayr moved up in the company, he retained his title, but Bobbie Cloke, a life-long Ladysmith resident, and long-time *Chronicle* sales rep slowly took over managing the paper. She was officially named publisher in 1997.

In a world of free-circulation community newspapers, the *Chronicle* remains, as it was 90 years ago: a paid circulation publication.

While the forest industry continues to be the area's predominant industry, a group of community visionaries have helped turn Chemainus and Ladysmith into historical tourist attractions, thus securing a future for the towns and for the paper that serves them.

LAKE COWICHAN GAZETTE

We only had the one office then, three years ago in June of 1995, when longtime Vancouver Island newspaperman George Manning decided to open a new weekly in Lake Cowichan.

Manning's company, Small Town Press, had been looking at the area for some time. In the weeks before the first issue of the *Gazette* was printed on June 14, 1995, a lucky few were witness to the hectic but orderly birth of a newspaper. Recollection of the days leading up to that first issue is, understandably, vague.

Someone figured out how to work the new coffee machine and was brewing the first pot as the movers were busy trying to figure out where to put all the furniture.

We were strangers to each other then, talking about spending time getting to know each other. The phone rang and one or another of our first customers stopped in. Conversations were put on hold, sleeves were rolled up, there'd be time for casual chit-chat later, wouldn't there? Looking back, those were the quiet days. Somehow amid the cacophony of our first week, we managed to design, sell and write a first issue. By then there was no looking back.

In three short years we've grown, adding pages, staff and floor space. We've met, and been embraced by, our new community. No easy task when you live in a small town that measures its locals by how many quarter-centuries they've lived here. And it's been fun. None of us who work here knew just what to expect. Since our first meeting, countless conversations have gone unfinished — interrupted by the never-ending rhythm of putting out a newspaper. In our paper's short life, we've gone from a freebie paper to paid publication — a rare feat for newspapers.

Something happened along the way. Having raised the paper from infancy, the people who work here have become more than our individual titles. Our production/office manager, Heather Roberts, brought a high-tech history with a national satellite company to the job. A big-city girl, Heather is still adapting to the many quirks of living in a small town. Dennis Skalicky, our publisher, came from a larger-market paper with an extensive background in sales. And he's still asking himself why. Our editor, Jim Zeeben, was hired because he could fill a newshole and because he was in the right place at the right time. As we have grown, so has our staff.

Along the way, we have embraced the spirit of the industry, becoming newspapermen and women, and looking forward to the changes and challenges that each new week will bring.

LAKE COWICHAN, LAKE NEWS

When Susan Lowe was 21 and agreed to move west with her parents in the mid-1980s, she never dreamt it would be a move that would completely change her life.

"My dad was a career newspaperman. One day he reads that a Lake Cowichan paper was up for sale and the next thing I know we're moving here."

Lowe spent several months helping her parents get going and then moved back east to finish her education.

Her mom and dad, Ron and Sheila Kenyon, were not the first to own the *News*. The newspaper started more as a flyer in 1958 when co-editors Irene Ardley and Adelaine Anderson wrote about the IWA, church picnics and community events.

The paper changed hands a couple of times more before it became a legacy for the Kenyon family.

"I kind of just fell into the business," Lowe says. "I didn't really plan it, but I had been helping out my dad since I was 12 and the newspaper business had become second nature to me."

Beginning first as a reporter and eventually becoming editor was a fairly smooth transition. It wasn't until her mother became ill and subsequently died that Lowe began to really feel the pressure of running a paper.

"My mom was sick and I had all these new responsibilities. It was a real tough time."

But Lowe weathered the storm and, with help from her husband Jamie Lowe, who quit his job as a car salesman to help run the advertising side of things, she has managed increase local subscriptions and attention.

"I really like to sink my teeth into a good journalistic story," she says. "I've always thought my real talents lay in writing fiction. But investigative journalism is just as much fun."

"Of course we are still a community paper and we have people to serve," she says. "But don't expect us to only tell good news stories. Because as we grow as a community, you can bet there will be plenty of bad news to report."

In 1996, the *News* was bought by the Thomson chain, which then sold to Southam in 1998. But you can bet Lowe is on the news beat, especially now that she has more time to devote to the editorial side of things.

LANTZVILLE LOG

Lantzville is an historic coal mining community outside Nanaimo. It has been 50 years since the last coal was taken out of the ground here, but a few mine workers still live in the area.

The *Lantzville Log* got its start back in about 1948 as a publication for the short-lived Lantzville Chamber of Commerce.

Over the years, the *Log* has been run by the Ratepayers and later, the Community Association took it under their respective wing and turned out about eight duplicator-printed, one-page issues a year. The *Log* has had its current newspaper format since 1978 and printed 12 issues a year since 1979.

The *Log* is mailed free of charge to every household and business in the Lantzville postal area. The population of Lantzville is currently 3,600, but because of population growth in the region that number changes almost daily.

—Wanda Cullen

NANAIMO BULLETIN

 Ten years ago, Nanaimo homeowners discovered a new newspaper in their mailbox.

The *Nanaimo Bulletin* arrived on the scene May 2, 1988 as part of the expanding family of Vancouver Island-owned Island Publishers.

With community papers in Courtenay, Parksville, Ladysmith, Duncan, Goldstream and Sidney, the time was right for Island Publishers to move into Nanaimo.

Now Island Publishers has grown to 16 publications.

Planting the idea for the *News Bulletin* was long-time Nanaimo newspaper executive Roy Linder.

"The daily paper had little circulation and the weekly's advertising

Photo by Merv Unger, Nanaimo News Bulletin

was too expensive," says the *News Bulletin* publisher. "We knew we could offer Nanaimo advertisers a shopping guide newspapers that would fit their needs exactly." And that it did.

A small, two-room office on Wilgress Road housed the first employees: Linder, advertising manager Tom Thomas and editor Merv Unger. Ignoring remarks that it would never succeed, the *Bulletin* continued to grow.

Bill Moore, who was on contract with his company Mid Island Flyers, was brought on as circulation manager and Cathy Donald became office manager. She's back at the *News Bulletin* for her third time.

The ad department then doubled when Mark MacDonald was brought on board. Production and presswork was done at Island Publisher's Ladysmith plant.

The premiere issue of Nanaimo's first tabloid newspaper was 16 pages with a full-colour front page featuring Miss Nanaimo contestants Melinda Borbandy and Julie Turner: The press run was 24,000.

Today it has grown to average of more than 48 pages with a circulation of 31,200 and a delivery network of 260 carriers from Yellowpoint and Gabriola Island to Lantzville and Nanoose. Continued growth led to a need for a larger office and in December 1989 the *Bulletin* moved to its present location in Terminal Park.

It didn't take long to realize that Nanaimo readers wanted more news in the product and the *Bulletin* responded with expanded city coverage. Published solely on Mondays, the paper branched out to twice a week June 2, 1994.

A staff of three has now grown to 25 employees.

"I can't thank enough the dedicated staff that we have had at the *Bulletin* over these years," says Linder. "And to come as far as we have in such a short period of time is most gratifying. It's almost hard to believe. We must have been doing something right."

—Chris Hamlyn

NANAIMO, HARBOUR CITY STAR

The *Harbour City Star*, a thrice-weekly community newspaper (circulation 33,500), serving central Vancouver Island, was launched December 3, 1996 by Thomson Newspapers. The *Star* joined Thomson's other Nanaimo publication, the *Nanaimo Daily News*, following a $1.3-million investment in the Nanaimo newspapers by Thomson. About half that amount was spent on new technology, including a Mac-based front-end system for both papers.

Both the *Star* and *Daily News* are published from the same office building on McCullough Road in Nanaimo. The *Star's* editor is Lynn Welburn. The paper is published Tuesday, Thursday and Saturday.

In 1998, the *Star* became property of Southam Publishing (B.C.) Ltd. following Southam's purchase of several Vancouver Island newspapers, including the *Daily News* and *Victoria Times-Colonist*.

Photo by Craig Hodge.

OAK BAY NEWS

Currently part of the Island Publishers chain of community newspapers on Vancouver Island, the *Oak Bay News* has a presence in the community which dates back almost a quarter of a century. The *Oak Bay News* started on October 23, 1974 as the independently owned *Oak Bay Star*, serving readership in the municipality of Oak Bay in Greater Victoria.

Running the *Star* was publisher Dan Heffernan and general manager Jim Borsman. John Thomson was both editor and photographer of the tab paper.

In 1987 Tony and Elizabeth Kant purchased the *Star* from John Hoole and Diane Gault.

Kant and his wife Elizabeth remained as co-publishers of the *Star* from 1987 through 1989, though they had sold the business within a year. Island Publishers Ltd. owner David Black, an Oak Bay resident, bought the *Star* from the Kants in May 1988, but the Kants stayed on to run the paper for another year, leaving in December 1989. Sales rep Ray Daniel took over as publisher and reporter Heather Bremner was promoted to editor. Bremner's tenure came to an end in June 1990 when Ken Faris was appointed editor.

Another change took place that October when James Manning was named *News* publisher. Manning remained in that position until May 1992, until Bob Black succeeded him.

Faris had departed two months earlier giving way to new editor John Balough. The *Star* became the *News* in February 1993 and Jamie Gripich, a news reporter since 1990, took over as editor in that same month. Nancy MacDonald succeeded him in April 1993. Black remained as publisher until February 1994 when Blair Cooke-Dallin took over that position, but by mid-April he was gone and sales rep Lisa Hopkins became associate publisher. A month later Tony Kant, who had been editing the *Peninsula News Review* for the News Group chain, was back in Oak Bay as both publisher and editor.

His second stay lasted less than a year. By March 1995 Carol Bailey had been installed as publisher and David Lennam as editor. Bailey and Lennam had previously worked for the News Group's Victoria and Regional *News* editions.

The *News* today has a circulation of 9,300 on its Wednesday run and 104,000 for its Friday product (a collective publication of all seven News Group community papers in Victoria). The Wednesday edition is delivered free to every home in Oak Bay.

Under current publisher Carol Bailey the *News* has regained some of its old strength, growing in the last three years from a paper averaging less than 20 pages to one that produces 32 pages every Wednesday. The *News* has won several provincial and national newspaper association awards. The *News* is a major player in civic activities, initiating and leading several local festivals and community events, as well as remaining chiefly involved in the June Oak Bay Tea Party and Tea Gardens. In recent years, the *News* and its readers started new annual events like The Great Cookie Extravaganza and a public Christmas party for the neighborhood, putting the community back into community newspaper in Oak Bay.

—*David Lennam*

PARKSVILLE QUALICUM BEACH NEWS

 All papers have to start somewhere, and the *Parksville Qualicum Beach News* started small, as a 16-page shopper on June 22, 1982.

Of course, back then, the *News* wasn't known as the *News*. It was the *Parksville Qualicum Beach Weekly Advertiser*, a fledgling periodical consisting mainly of ads, as well as a few columns, submitted articles and features.

It began not during a boom period, but in a time of recession. This takes a bit of explanation, because it might otherwise seem like an odd decision by Island Publishers Ltd., its parent company.

The *Parksville-Qualicum Beach Progress*, a newspaper, which served the area since 1948, closed down in April 1982, meaning the *Arrowsmith Star* was the only community paper serving Parksville and Qualicum Beach.

When Island Publishers put out its feelers, the company found plenty of businesses in the area willing to lend their support to a new paper, including Vancouver Island grocery store chain Quality Foods, which has remained a huge *News* advertiser.

The *Weekly Advertiser* changed its name to the *Parksville-Qualicum Beach News-Advertiser* and Roy Linder, the paper's first publisher, remembers struggling in these formative times, when his paper, working with a skeleton staff, fought to establish itself in District 69.

Then, as now, the paper was distributed to its main coverage areas, including Parksville, Qualicum Beach and some nearby rural communities, for free.

The key to scraping by at the beginning was the support of advertisers, not the editorial content, Linder says.

"There wasn't any news forte at the time," he says. "We just got a lot of assistance for the other merchants that didn't want to work with the other paper."

After a couple of years the *News-Advertiser* began increasing its editorial focus, adding more news stories in response to public demand. Though the paper had solid backing from its advertisers, it was still a fledgling production that had to stumble through countless trials and tribulations.

"We were not the number-one paper in town, we were still fighting for our lives with the *Arrowsmith Star*," recalls Linder, who now sits at the helm of another Island Publishers vehicle, the *Nanaimo News Bulletin*.

Of course, nutty community newspaper personalities go hand in hand with community newspapers, and the *News* was no exception. In its early years, characters such as editor Tony Kant patrolled the newsroom. Kant, who always infuriated someone with his opinionated columns, was also noted for his weird manner of dress.

"I remember Tony Kant was really wild," Linder says, laughing. "Like, he'd have a pink shirt and an orange tie. Or no shirt at all."

According to one of his protégés, current *News* publisher Judi Thompson, Linder was also a bit of a character.

Generally pleasant in demeanor, the big guy wasn't afraid to exercise his vocal chords when someone messed up, says Thompson, who worked under the healthily-lunged head honcho when she started as an advertising representative in 1986.

"He had a big, thundering voice that used to scare the hell out of everybody," Thompson says. One of the biggest changes in the paper since she's joined has been its evolution from ad publication to newspaper.

"When I first started work in 1986, there was barely any editorial staff," Thompson says. "It was basically a sales advertising project; that was it."

At the time, an editor and part-time reporter handled the news load. Now, the paper sports three reporters, an assistant editor and an editor, all full-time.

Overall, in her time at the paper, Thompson has seen staff numbers grow from eight (six full-time and two part-time) to 28 (24 full-time; four part-time).

And finally, a note to any prospective visitors: never, ever refer to "Qualicum Beach" as "Qualicum" while speaking to town residents, unless you don't mind them running you down in their seniors' carts.

—*Chris Miller*

PARKSVILLE-QUALICUM BEACH MORNING SUN

The *Parksville-Qualicum Beach Morning Sun* published its first issue on November 23, 1994 under the banner the *Paper*. Most of its staff were former employees of the *Arrowsmith Star*, which had been bought and subsequently closed by Island Publishers earlier that year, so Thomson Newspapers found a pre-assembled staff roster to start their new publication.

Under original publisher Richard Odo and editor John Carter, the paper gained a toehold in the competitive Parksville-Qualicum region. Originally a twice-weekly newspaper, it changed to once-weekly in July 1996 to coincide with a change of name, design and layout.

In 1998, the *Morning Sun* gained a measure of national notoriety following its exposure of the Paul Reitsma scandal. The Parksville-Qualicum MLA was caught sending letters to the editor under false names, and subsequently lied about doing so when confronted by the *Morning Sun's* editor.

A recall campaign followed the release of the story, and Reitsma narrowly avoided being the first Canadian politician ever recalled by his constituents when he resigned on June 23, 1998.

The paper was acquired from Thomson Newspapers by Southam in the summer of 1998 as part of the Vancouver Island group.

The *Morning Sun* has a circulation of 17,417, and covers the area of Vancouver Island stretching between Nanoose Bay (just north of Nanaimo) in the south to Deep Bay in the north.

—*Rory McGrath*

PORT HARDY, NORTH ISLAND GAZETTE

Considerable doubt has been raised as to whether the first newspaper to serve northern Vancouver Island was really a newspaper.

Published in Vancouver, it was distributed in Port Hardy, then known as Hardy Bay. It had all the appearances of a newspaper, local as well as international news and a minimum of advertising. However, it had ties to an alleged group of real estate swindlers who succeeded in luring many people, to their subsequent sorrow, into what was vividly described as a pastoral paradise. Called the *Hardy Bay News*, it was first published in November 1913, and the few copies in existence indicate it continued for about a year.

In 1946 Ron Shuker, an Alert Bay merchant with a tremendous sense of community responsibility, began publication of the *Pioneer Journal*. It was a stapled mimeographed sheet, which, considering Shuker's other involvement as an alderman and leader of the Board of Trade, came out with remarkable regularity.

Shuker continued the publication until his death in 1960. His widow and two sons, Ronald and Reginald, continued on and soon installed a Multilith press. Ronald left two years later to go to journalism school and Reginald carried on alone until he too left the community in 1963.

Urged by the Alert Bay Board of Trade, Neville Shanks, who had been the editor of the *Campbell River Courier*, moved to the community in 1965 and began publication of the *North Island Gazette*, a tabloid printed in Courtenay.

Alert Bay had, until this time, been the commercial centre of northern Vancouver Island. Situated on Cormorant Island, a small island off the northeast coast of Vancouver Island, this continued as long as communication was mainly by sea. However, with the opening of roads and increased air service, economic activity began to be centred in Port McNeill and Port Hardy, two communities on Vancouver Island itself.

This brought about moving the paper, in 1957, to Port Hardy.

From the beginning a marginal family operation, the paper continued this way until 1970, when announcement of the opening of the huge Utah Construction and Mining Company Ltd. copper mine near Port Hardy gave the local economy a surge that in many ways approached a boom.

The paper's fortunes received another boost when it concluded arrangements to do the printing for Utah and the Rayonnier Canada pulp mill at nearby Port Alice. A job printing plant was installed to take care of this work as well as that for the many other businesses moving into the rapidly growing area.

The paper was still basically a family operation up until this point in history. Neville Shanks was publisher and editor; his wife Regina advertising manager; son Roland was business manager and photographer and looked after the mechanics of preparing the publication for the printer's camera. Another son, Hugh, took care of the job printing. Even after 30 years, area residents remember the family.

In 1974, Neville Shanks was bought out by son Roland and Ross Mavis, who stepped down as secretary-treasurer of the school board to become a partner. The younger Shanks said the next decade were the "glory years" as the newspaper won awards in all categories at the BCYCNA convention, even receiving best all-round paper in its category at the Canadian Community Newspapers Association convention. One year, they took the whole staff to Vancouver for the convention. "It was an excellent, excellent staff in my estimation. We tried our best to compensate them and treat them accordingly."

The owners acquired the latest technology to help put the paper out. They took pride in the product and were actively involved in putting out the paper.

Weekly one-hour staff meetings were held with no set agenda. It was an opportunity to iron out any problems, but most of the time they sat down with coffee and told a few jokes. "If we couldn't solve a problem, at least we cleared the air," says Shanks.

Photo by Terry Kruger, Powell River News

There were the usual stories that reporters, as observers, cover: a young arsonist burns down Robert Scott School; a Hughes 18 crashes on the runway at Port Hardy Airport. However, the paper, as community booster, also made news. One year, they decided to push for a long-promised paved highway from Sayward to Port McNeill. The newspaper considered the long ferry ride from Kelsey Bay to Beaver Cove and alternate controlled logging road as the main economic drawback to the economy, says Shanks. "The road had been pushed aside. After trying for so long, the effort was at a low ebb. We decided to give it one more kick at the cat."

They kicked off the campaign with a front-page open letter to the highways minister and paraphernalia adorned with logos of a half-eaten carrot designed by Mavis. The government reissued contracts it had cancelled shortly before and within two years, the modern highway was built. A sculpture of a half-eaten carrot still marks the terminus of the highway in Port Hardy.

Shanks didn't attend the ribbon cutting by Premier W.A.C. Bennett. "It didn't impress me. There was a lot of fanfare and not really much getting done. We forced them, they built the road, the deed was done."

Shortly after, B.C. Ferries constructed a ferry terminal in Port Hardy at Bear Cove as the southern terminus of a new run to Prince Rupert. The resulting surge in tourism was fantastic, says Shanks, and new fish processors joined established Seafood Products in Hardy Bay.

However, the Port McNeill Chamber of Commerce was suspicious, asking Shanks what the newspaper stood to gain by the campaign. It invested $5,000 with nothing promised in return, except to see the economy of the area improve and the newspaper with it.

Ironically, the highway stopped at the foot of Douglas Street next to the newspaper's office at the northeastern tip of the Island. One day as Shanks stared out his window, he noticed a crowd gathering at the government wharf. Running out with his camera, he discovered a canoe had capsized and the locals were standing around simply watching.

Noticing a kid frantically trying to start the outboard motor on his skiff, Shanks ran down and choked the motor. The engine kicked in and the rescuers arrived just in time. From that day forward, whenever anyone sarcastically commented on Shanks' habit of staring out the window of his office to the beautiful Queen Charlotte Straits and Coast Mountains beyond, he defensively replied he was keep his eye open for any rescue work.

Fittingly, Shanks and Mavis were founding members of the Kinsmen Club, which set up ambulance service to the community. The system received such high praise that within six months of its inception, the B.C. Ambulance Service was formed to provide provincial coverage.

Over a cup of coffee one day, Shanks, Neil Crook and others came up with the idea for a July celebration of the three main industries, fishing, logging and mining. The organizing committee enlisted the help of other groups, each one sponsoring an event.

In the 1980s the *Gazette* was sold to E.W. Bickle, publishers of the *Comox District Free Press*. It also went with the Bickle holdings to Thomson Newspapers in a buy-out in the late 1980s.

One dark night in 1992, Thomson announced the closure of the newspaper. However, publisher Rod Sluggett called contacts in David Black's Island Publishers, who bought the equipment and reopened the newspaper the next day with fewer staff and no print shop. The newspaper is once again a tabloid after being broadsheet for many years.

Despite the closure of the Island Copper Mine in 1996 and the uncertainties in the logging and fishing industries, the newspaper has continued to serve the communities of the North Island.

Though the ownership has gone from an independent to a chain, albeit family and staff-owned, the tradition of community service has carried on over the years. The *Gazette* instituted a Christmas hamper program in the mid-1980s.

Various publishers have organized Filomi Days and sat on chamber and economic development committees.

Former owner Shanks, who returned to the North Island after an absence, says a revelation came to him in later years. "From the newspaper, you could see what needed to be done and who was doing it. I realized nobody else would do it if you don't do it. So give it a shot."

POWELL RIVER NEWS/TOWN CRIER

 Throughout its 90-odd years of existence, Powell River has probably had far more than its fair share of local publications.

The *Powell River News* made its entry in 1927 when T.W. Green was its publisher. He sold it to L.C. Way in 1943, and he in turn sold it to Al Alsgard in 1945.

In 1970 the operations of the *Powell River News* were sold to a group of Winnipeg investors headed by Dr. T. Ethans. The sale included the *Penninsula Times* in Sechelt and the *Town Crier* at Powell River.

The newspaper, *News/Town Crier*, continued to thrive and grow as a twice-a-week publication through the 1970s and into the 1980s. During that period, the newspaper received numerous provincial and national honors, including being named Best All Round Newspaper by the B.C. & Yukon Community Newspapers Association (BCYCNA) in 1982, winning the Canadian Community Newspapers Association (CCNA) prize for Best Front Page in 1986 and CCNA's Best Feature Photo prize in 1988. That tradition continues in the 1990s: the paper placed second in the BCYCNA General Excellence Awards in 1992 and won prizes for feature writing in subsequent years.

The *Powell River News* is published on Wednesdays. It switched from broadsheet to tabloid format in January 1998.

The *Town Crier* is now published on Sundays, in a tabloid format, a move made in April 1997. Until then, the *Town Crier* was published each Monday as a broadsheet newspaper.

POWELL RIVER PEAK

The *Powell River Peak* newspaper was launched in November 1995. Its parent company, Peak Publishing Ltd., is a joint venture, co-owned by Carmil Enterprises Ltd., a Powell River family company owned by Joyce and Don Carlson, their sons Brent and Shane, and Lower Mainland Publishing Ltd., which owns or is a partner in 33 newspapers in B.C. and Washington State.

Some 9,000 copies of the tabloid newspaper with a process-colour front page are distributed every week from Saltery Bay to Lund, including Texada Island.

Within the municipality, *Peaks* are delivered from house to house by carrier. The *Peak* carrier force, including youngsters and adults, numbers more than 100.

Rural readers, with the exception of three carrier routes, are delivered via drop boxes that are placed next to Canada Post mailboxes. Canada Post is used to deliver to every resident on Texada

Joyce Carlson, publisher, Powell River Peak, *1998*

Island. An area breakdown of delivery is provided each week and numbers are audited by an independent organization. The *Peak* has a staff of 10 people and several contributors. In 1998, the *Peak* received several newspaper industry awards. In the Suburban Newspapers of America competition, the newspaper received a first-place award for best editorial page cartoon and third-place award for best spot news photo. The contest was open to member newspapers in Canada and the United States.

At the B.C. & Yukon Community Newspapers Association annual meeting in Penticton in May 1998 the *Peak* was named runner-up in its circulation category of 6,500 -12,999, came second for best historical writing and second for best feature photo in the under-10,000 circulation category. In addition, an honourable mention was received for best black and white ad design.

SAANICH NEWS

The *Saanich News* is a twice-weekly community newspaper delivered to 32,000 homes. Delivered on Wednesdays and Fridays, the *Saanich News* reaches residents stretching from the rural farmlands of Prospect Lake to the rugged coves of Ten-Mile Point.

The *Saanich News* opened its doors in 1986. Two years later it merged with the *Gordon Head News* and established itself as a strong voice in the region's largest and fastest growing community.

The Municipality of Saanich is home to more than 100,000 residents living in mostly single-family dwellings with incomes ranging from average to high-end. The municipality boasts the most parkland in the Greater Victoria area and maintains a unique blend of urban growth dotted with pockets of rural countryside.

The *Saanich News* serves a community that takes pride in itself and is vocally active on issues that affect Saanich. With this in mind, the newspaper strives to provide comprehensive coverage on topics of importance to Saanich's diverse range of residents.

With a blend of hard news, community, municipal politics, entertainment and sports stories, the *Saanich News* covers issues that touch all Saanich residents.

Sidney, Peninsula News Review

The *Sidney, Peninsula News Review* was first published on December 13, 1912, called simply the *Sidney Review*. It was initiated by a group of shareholders, including J.J. White, a prominent citizen in Sidney until his death in 1958.

Beginning as an eight-page tabloid, the *Review* expanded to broadsheet in 1919, although its news and photo content was meager. Successive publishers have run the paper over the years — A. Emery Moore, Alfred Cunningham, Felix Fernari, Walter Wakefield, Hugh McIntyre, F.C.E Ford, Clare Rivers and George Manning to name a few.

Today the *Sidney, Peninsula News Review* is owned by Island Publishers and enjoys a healthy and growing readership.

Sooke News Mirror

The *Sooke News Mirror*, which serves a bucolic coastal community on the shores of the Strait of Juan de Fuca 35 kilometres southwest of Victoria, has been operating for 39 years.

In that time, the paper has had five different owners, three different names and only one office manager, Harla Eve, a Sooke girl born and bred, who joined the paper in January 1975 and still presides over the front desk and the all-important accounts receivable.

The secret to lasting 23 years in one job, says Harla, is the fact that she has had so many different bosses: "I never got a chance to get tired of any of them."

When Harla joined the paper, the publisher was Bud Pauls, a former military public relations man, who bought the paper from the founding publisher, Maurice Tozer, in the early 70s.

The *Mirror* had first started reflecting the views of a then-remote coastal community on January 14, 1959 when Tozer produced a weekly six-page, mimeographed edition, which he called the *Grapevine*.

He appealed to community organizations to send in news items "because my budget doesn't run to salaried reporters." He set up a

Left to right: Paul Stenner, John Damgaard, John Manning, 1978.

newspaper office in a converted pump house on his property and typed out the paper on a stencil, which he would take to Victoria to be mimeographed.

As the circulation grew the name was changed to the *Mirror* and Pauls who operated it until 1980 purchased the paper. He sold it to editorial employee Donna James who was publisher until 1983 when she sold it to John Arnett, a former *Vancouver Sun* reporter, communications consultant and senior government bureaucrat who says he realized the dream of many journalists to own their own newspaper.

Arnett recalls that George Manning, then publisher of the *Goldstream Gazette* tipped him off that the paper was for sale.

"When I asked George why he didn't buy the paper himself he told me the current owner was asking far too much money for it, the community was depressed because logging and commercial fishing had hit the skids and there was a limited number of businesses to buy advertising.

"George told me that he felt the overhead of running a paper was too great to make any money and said I would probably go broke in a couple of years. But my wife Norma and I decided to mortgage our house and buy anyway, paying the full asking price. Fortunately my wife was working, so I didn't have to pay myself a salary for a number of years and that certainly helped the bottom line."

In hindsight Manning would probably admit that he was wrong because Sooke was to boom as an affordable bedroom community of Victoria with the population, and the number of businesses doubling in the next five or six years. Today the area has a population of 12,000 and is one of the fastest growing in the region.

The paper's circulation jumped from 1,600 paid to 3,500 free circulation a few months after Arnett took over. He made the change in response to other free papers being printed in Victoria circulated in the community. There were concerns by local advertisers that the *Mirror* wasn't reaching enough people as a paid paper.

The Arnetts published the paper until March 1992 when they sold it to David Black and the paper became part of the Victoria News Group, changing its name to the *Sooke News Mirror*.

First News Group publisher was Reg Cowie followed by Michael Turnpenny (now publisher of *Monday* magazine). In 1996, Rod Sluggett moved from the publishing the *North Island Gazette* in Port Hardy to the *News Mirror*.

The *Sooke News Mirror* currently has a free circulation of 5,200. It averages a healthy 32 pages each week and is produced with all of the bells and whistles of the computer age — a far cry from that rainy January day in 1959 when the first publisher typed out his newspaper on a stencil in a converted pump house in his back yard.

TOFINO-UCLUELET WESTERLY NEWS

The *Tofino-Ucluelet Westerly News* can perhaps lay claim to being the only newspaper printed on Canada's Pacific Coast, for its headquarters are located on the ocean's edge in Ucluelet on Vancouver Island.

It serves well known Long Beach, Tofino and Port Albion. Today the area, famous for Pacific Rim National Park, attracts large numbers of tourists from all parts of the world.

Although a direct line cannot be drawn because there have been gaps in publication over the years, the paper's precursor and first in the area was the *Tofino-Ucluelet Press*, established in 1958 by George and Mae Simpson. Today the *Tofino-Ucluelet Westerly News* thrives along with the coastal region it serves.

VICTORIA, MONDAY MAGAZINE

A while back, *Monday* staff stopped correcting people who said, "I like your newspaper." Like we say on the cover, *Monday* is a magazine. But I've heard it referred to so often as a newspaper, sometimes I wonder if we've got it right. In many ways, it looks like a newspaper. It's printed on newsprint, it comes out weekly and it's folded down the middle — just like a newspaper. Most magazines come out monthly, they're generally bound or stapled and printed on glossy paper or other quality paper stock. So why do we call it *Monday* when it's printed on Wednesday and distributed on Thursday?

The name can be credited to our founders, Gene Miller and Bill Barringer. Back in 1975, they decided to distribute their brand new product on Monday because it was the one day of the week not fully covered by the other Victoria papers. It seemed like a good idea at the time, but they quickly discovered that readers and advertisers preferred a publication that appeared toward the end of the week. Factors like evening shopping hours, paydays, more time for entertainment, leisure — reading a weekly magazine. So they switched to Thursday, but they kept the name.

Once you establish an identity among your customers, it's tough to change the name of any business. So we're stuck with the name and with explaining the Monday-Thursday contradiction a few hundred times a year. Looking on the bright side, *Monday* is still a good name for our publication. We write many of the articles on Monday and it's the beginning of the workweek, representing a fresh start (hopefully), after a weekend of rest and relaxation. How's that for a silk purse?

Now, why do we call it a magazine? Let's start by looking at newspapers. Their mandate is to present the news — usually daily or weekly — in a straightforward, easy-to-read, neutral writing style. Newspapers also include separate columns and editorial that present writer's viewpoints, or the position of the publication. News articles

David Black, then premier Mike Harcourt, early 1990s.

are generally restricted to "just the facts," leaving opinion to columnists and editorial writers. A newspaper is generally discarded after
one brief or leisurely sitting. Particularly in the case of a daily, there
will be another one on the way tomorrow morning.

A magazine is more of a collective of stories, an eclectic mix, perhaps to be scanned quickly at coffee break on Thursday and read
more leisurely at home over the weekend. Certainly, a magazine is
expected to last longer than a newspaper, whether it's just the end of
the week to consult the calendar, or as part of your permanent collection of favourite back issues.

From an insider's perspective, a magazine is different from a newspaper in both form and content. Despite some similarities, we strive
for a more stylistic, graphic presentation — in both the ads and the
editorial articles and photographs. That's form. In content, we attempt to present more than the news — and often less. We don't have
the space or the resources to cover everything that's going on in our
city, province or world. So we try to choose a few topics and areas of
interest and write about them differently. We look for a unique approach — perhaps it's an issue or person or event you've never seen
discussed before, or discussed quite that way. We try to present detail

and analysis, instead of just reporting what happened this week.

A good newspaper article will tell you what the premier said. A good magazine article will tell you about his thinning hair, his body language and his impeccably-tailored, ash-gray, three-piece suit. It should also set what he said in context with what he said or did last week and with other perspectives. What we're looking for in magazine writing is "point of view," a shade less definitive than opinion. And we expect any viewpoints expressed to be well informed. If a writer hasn't put extensive research and thought into the subject, his or her opinion is of no more value than the casual comments you get in a beer parlour.

So in some ways, we look and feel like a newspaper. But we still think the product we present to you every week is a magazine. Maybe we're somewhere in the middle. Which may not be a bad place to be if we can borrow some of the best elements of both forms. Now if we can only convince people to start calling the fifth day of the week *Monday*.

—*Sid Tafler*

VICTORIA NEWS

In 1985, David Black, the owner of Black Press and numerous papers in the Interior of British Columbia, moved to Greater Victoria with his family and made it his home. Black saw a great deal of potential for existing and new community newspapers as Vancouver Island began to grow both in population and economically. It was at this point that he began working with George Manning to build Island Publishers on the Island.

George Manning, as president of Island Publishers, took the company from 18 employees to over 400 during his tenure. This arrangement lasted for over 10 years before Manning decided it was time for new challenges. After a short-lived retirement he began purchasing papers in Lake Cowichan and the Interior.

As president of Island Publishers, Manning found and hired publishers who truly understood the community involvement required for a successful community paper. Black and Manning had a simple mandate: community newspapers must be community members.

They were committed to delivering the news community by community and this network of community papers allowed them to support each community through good times and bad times.

Victoria was an interesting anomaly for a community paper. Publisher David Darwin worked closely with *Victoria Star* editor Vaughn Cocke to shape the *Victoria News* in a manner that recognized the urban qualities of Victoria while retaining the sensibilities of a community paper. The early 80s saw a lot of change for the *Victoria Star* including a brief period when the papers were called the *Weeklies*.

In 1990, a regional paper was developed in order to give a perspective on the entire Greater Victoria region. George Manning recognized that local residents were not just Victorians, they were Greater Victorians. This paper was run out of the *Victoria News* office and entitled *This Week*. It was delivered inside the *Goldstream Gazette*, the *Review*, the *Saanich/Gordon Head News*, *Oak Bay Star*, *Esquimalt News* and *Victoria Star*.

This Week had a regional overview of Greater Victoria while the *Victoria News* first section was specifically about Victoria and Victorians. The *Victoria News* was now able to address the needs of its readers by providing quality community information as well as regional coverage.

In 1992, Glenn Rogers took over the reins of Island Publishers, which now included over 13 papers on the Island. He was a Toronto refugee, like many current Victorians and brought with him a new edge to the *Victoria Star*, which included a change in both the look and the feel of the paper.

In 1992 Rogers worked with Palmer Jarvis and began marketing the Greater Victoria papers as the News Group and changed the names of the papers to reflect this new identity. The *Victoria News* was born. In 1995 six of the seven papers (*Victoria News, Peninsula News Review, Goldstream News Gazette, Esquimalt News, Oak Bay News* and *Saanich News*) in the region began twice-a-week delivery. The Wednesday *Victoria News* focused exclusively on the residents and activities of Victorians, while the Friday *Victoria News Weekend Edition* was common to all six papers and gave a broad perspective on all of Greater Victoria. Cindy Harnett, already editor of the *Victoria News*, became the regional editor for the *Weekend Edition*, driving both papers to reflect the urban, cultured environment they covered.

Photo by Chuck Russell.

Some extensive personnel changes also came in 1995. Jim Tighe, former vice-president of corporate planning for the Toronto Sun Corporation, joined Island Publishers as its president and James Manning, son of George Manning, became publisher of the *Victoria News*, bringing things full-circle. Both Manning and Tighe are Island boys who have worked all of their lives in papers beginning as carriers in their pre-teen years, gathering experience in virtually all areas until their final ascent into management.

Today the *Victoria News* is one of 16 News Group community papers delivered far and wide across Vancouver Island. The *Vic News*, as it is fondly called, reaches the doorsteps of over 26,000 homes, in addition to being available in drop boxes around the downtown Victoria core. Its beat stretches throughout the neighborhoods of Fairfield, James Bay, Fernwood and downtown Victoria.

Publishing in a tabloid format twice a week, the *Victoria News* stretches the boundaries of traditional community newspapers with an eclectic mix of hard-hitting municipal news, provincial and federal politics, arts and entertainment, investigative and lifestyles features in addition to a comprehensive sports section. The *Vic News* offers a marriage of local grassroots community coverage with cutting-edge urban news.

The *Weekend Edition*, the Friday edition of all of our Greater Victoria papers, is delivered every Friday to 104,000 households in Victoria, the Peninsula, Saanich, Oak Bay, Esquimalt, and the Western Communities. It covers a wide breadth of regional news, arts, entertainment, sports and features.

In addition to regular features, *Victoria News* has established some very popular supplements targetted to our diverse readership. A bi-annual Seniors Directory is distributed to 60,000 residents across Greater Victoria and explores the new active lifestyles of today's seniors and services available for those over 55. *Victoria News* includes a quarterly Fashion Supplement, a monthly West Coast Homes & Gardens feature and seasonal supplements on Gardening and Christmas all distributed through the *Weekend Edition* to the 104,000 households across Greater Victoria.

The most successful and best-loved supplement, however, is the *Victoria News Best of the City*. Each year local residents are asked to vote on everything from the best place to propose to the best daycare. Needless to say the paper receives calls from local and distant fans of this publication as early as January in order to request the next issue. The results from all 105 categories are published in a special July issue that includes Q&A with local celebrities, fun editorial and pictures of local businesses proudly displaying their plaque denoting their standing as one of the Best of the City.

The other outstanding issue that the *Victoria News* has received recognition for is a special Violence Supplement, printed shortly after Reena Virk was killed by local teenagers in 1997. Jim Tighe authorized the publishing of this supplement demonstrating solutions for young people, options for kids on the wrong track and success stories of teens who had turned themselves around. The centre of the supplement was simply a picture of local kids and their signatures pledging to stop the violence. The entire supplement was fully subsidized by Island Publishers, which in turn asked local businesses that would have advertised in the supplement to instead put that money towards local associations and programs helping today's youth.

It is that kind of diversity that has created a loyal following for the *Victoria News* and the *Victoria News Weekend Edition*.

—Cheryl Wirch-Ryckman

Lower Mainland / Southwest

TUESDAY EDITION

AdvanceNews

Vancouver ECHO

Chilliwack **TIMES**

60¢
at newsstand

Tuesday, September 15, 1998

A combined 60 Pages

The Aldergrove Star

3089 - 272nd Street ☆ Ph: (604) 856-8303 ☆ Fax: 856-5212
Web Site: www.aldstar.com ☆ E Mail: star@aldstar.com

Illegitimus non carborundum

WEDNESDAY, AUGUST 12, 1998

50 CENTS

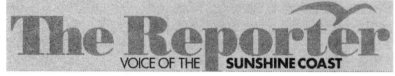

The Reporter

VOICE OF THE SUNSHINE COAST

THE

NOW

WESTENDER

ABBOTSFORD NEWS

John A. Bates, who was publishing a weekly newspaper in Mission, decided that Abbotsford, seven miles away across the Fraser River, should have its own newspaper, so he started the *Abbotsford Post* in 1906. Prior to this the Abbotsford area had been covered by the Mission newspaper.

The *Abbotsford Post* was short-lived under the ownership of Mr. Bates and in December 1922 Gerald H. Heller purchased the paper and it became known as the *Abbotsford, Sumas and Matsqui News*.

Situated in Abbotsford, the newspaper covered the areas of Sumas and Matsqui municipalities. Abbotsford district was incorporated as a village in 1927. With Mr. Heller at its helm, the newspaper published weekly and averaged six to eight pages.

In 1938 Heller sold the *News* to Lang Sands of New Westminster. Sands came to Abbotsford with newspaper training, having worked at Chilliwack until 1927 as assistant editor and later at the *Columbian* in New Westminster.

Sands' first project was to make the *News* an all-home print publication. Two years later the paper was eight pages of local news and produced entirely in the Abbotsford shop. Its circulation was over 1,000.

Jack Birt (Honorary Life Member of BCYCNA), Shirley Lashbrook (wife of 1978 CCNA president Lynn Lashbrook) and Cliff Hacker (publisher of M.S.A. News, Abbotsford) enjoy the Chinatown dinner sponsored by the Ford Motor Company.

In 1949 the *News* was sold to Cecil Hacker who came from the *Chilliwack Progress*. And in 1962 the Liverpool Daily Post and Echo Limited purchased the *News* and two neighbouring weeklies, the *Chilliwack Progress* and the *Fraser Valley Record* in Mission City. Hacker became president of the three publishing companies.

The *Abbotsford News* continues to be a strong presence in the community; in recent years it joined several Fraser Valley newspapers, including sister papers the *Hope Standard* and the *Chilliwack Progress*, as part of the Metro Valley Newspaper Group.

ABBOTSFORD/ MAPLE RIDGE-PITT MEADOWS/ CHILLIWACK, THE TIMES

The *Abbotsford Times* began publishing in 1984 as the *Teletimes* in Abbotsford and Chilliwack. The original publishers, the Wonnacott family, felt they could provide an alternative source of information for readers and a new opportunity for advertisers to markets dominated for years by Hacker Press.

In 1985 the format of the publication was changed to a tabloid and two editions, for the Upper-Fraser Valley and Central Valley, were published under the *Valley Times* nameplate.

In the spring of 1986 the Now Times Group was formed when Madison Venture Corporation, owners of four newspapers publishing under the *Now* nameplate, acquired controlling interest in the *Times*. Later that year the *Maple Ridge Times* began publishing and joined the *Chilliwack and Abbotsford-Clearbrook Times* as part of the seven newspapers in the group.

In May of 1990 the Now Times Group of newspapers, including the *Abbotsford Clearbrook Times*, were part of a major publication merger which formed Lower Mainland Publishing Limited (LMPL). This merger saw the acquisition of newspapers in Richmond and Delta plus the *Vancouver Courier*, and assets of the *North Shore News* and Now Times Group plus capital from the Southam Newspaper Group. Although Southam holds 49% of the new company, day-to-day management is still controlled by local interests. This local management autonomy allows LMPL to aggressively target markets in in-

Robert Bonner (Chair, B.C. Hydro), Dan Murray (Life Member BCYNA) and Gerry Freeman (publisher, Agassiz Harrison Advance), 1977.

dividual cities in newspapers and pre-printed insert sales and delivery. From an editorial standpoint editors and publishers have the ability to establish editorial style to best meet the needs of their community rather than being forced to produce "cookie cutter" products. As part of the merger LMPL set up a marketing organization responsible for providing advertisers the opportunity to purchase space in a group of 22 newspapers either owned by or affiliated with them. The new organization was referred to as the Vancouver Area Newspaper Network (VanNet).

The rapid growth experienced by the *Abbotsford-Clearbrook Times* through 1989 and 1990 allowed establishment of a second issue in the fall of 1991. The *Times* now provides twice-a-week full market coverage in Abbotsford, Matsqui and Mission.

In 1992 the District of Matsqui celebrated its centennial with the *Times* playing an important role in promoting events throughout the year. This established the *Times* as a credible source of information in the community and launched a new era of growth for the newspaper.

In late 1994 the communities of Abbotsford and Matsqui held a referendum to choose a name for the newly amalgamated city. The *Times* once again took a leadership role by making a name change to

Chuck McKnight and Cliff Hacker, August 1978.

the *Abbotsford Times* prior to the vote. In this way the newspaper made a clear editorial statement to the community regarding its choice for the name of the new city.

The *Times'* commitment to the community has been one reason for its growth and 1995 was an example of this when it became a major media sponsor of the Western Canada Summer Games.

The *Times* prides itself on being market driven and responsive to changes in the community and needs of the readers and advertisers.

AGASSIZ-HARRISON OBSERVER

The *Agassiz-Harrison Observer* has been published since March 1990, when it was launched by publisher Chris Nickless and his wife Val. Although initially published by the couple for a short period in 1982, the *Observer* was revived in early 1990. Rick Froese became the editor at this time after working one year with the *Delta Optimist* as a sports reporter. Serving the communities of Agassiz, Harrison Hot Springs and Harrison Mills, and the Seabird Island and Chehalis native bands, the *Observer* expanded in the spring of 1992 to communities south of the Fraser River, reaching Rosedale, Popcum and Bridal Falls. In July 1997, the *Observer* was sold to Black Press Ltd., which also owns neighbouring community newspapers *Chilliwack Progress*, *Hope Standard*, *Mission City Record* and *Abbotsford News*. While a new permanent publisher was being sought, *Mission City Record* publisher and editor Don Button became interim publisher of the *Observer*.

The *Observer* welcomed Andrew Yeates as publisher and wife Lisa McKnight-Yeates as editor in December 1997. Together they brought extensive experience in community newspapers, having spent more than 25 years in the business at newspapers in British Columbia and Ontario. Through these times of transition, Froese remains on staff as reporter and photographer.

ALDERGROVE STAR

The community of Aldergrove is home to a number of weekly newspaper incarnations, under different owners and publication names since 1957. In the summer of 1966, the *Aldergrove Star*, then known as the *Echo*, was purchased by the Langmann family. They continue to own and operate the paper to this day.

Rudy Langmann had been a journeyman carpenter, but a serious back injury from a fall had hospitalized him in 1965. On the advice of physicians, Rudy searched for a career change. His brother-in-law, Cesare Tofini, had just purchased the Italian language weekly, *L'eco d'Italia* in Vancouver. Cesare told Rudy that *L'eco d'Italia's* former owner, Pietro Mori, also had a weekly newspaper in Aldergrove that he wished to sell before returning to Toronto.

Rudy and wife Inge both had strong interests and education in literature dating back to their youth in Denmark, and decided that such a business opportunity was ideal for a working couple. A deal was made, and they moved their home and three young boys from Yarrow to Aldergrove.

Rudy and Inge worked vigorously to understand and know the community, and to learn the craft. They retained another former owner, Alfred Flamond, as the advertising salesperson, and set to build up the slim broadsheet. One of the first changes made was to rename the paper the *Aldergrove Star*, as the couple didn't want to "echo" anyone. They have also changed the format several times, al-

Publisher Rudy Langmann in front of the Aldergrove Star *heritage building, 1998.*

though the tabloid format has remained constant for the past 15 years.

Their eldest son, Kurt, joined the business full-time in 1973, and is currently the editor. Inge Langmann is manager of advertising sales, and publisher Rudy Langmann has forged the paper's successful Internet edition since 1997 with the help of second son Franz. Development of the Internet edition is ongoing, but as of spring 1998 receives over 60,000 visits per month by readers from around the globe.

The backbone remains the newsprint edition, however, which also underwent a major transformation in 1997 when the family decided to change it from paid-circulation distribution to free. Over 9,000 homes in Langley and Abbotsford municipalities now receive the *Aldergrove Star* weekly, in the area between the Canada-U.S. border to the Fraser River, and Mount Lehman Road to Otter Road.

BOWEN ISLAND UNDERCURRENT

The *Undercurrent* has served Bowen Island since 1975. The paper was started by Pat Weaver, a young Island resident, who felt that the

Photo by Brian Giebelhaus, Burnaby News Leader.

600 or so permanent residents deserved a community forum that would document current happenings, announce events, and provide a place for individual opinions through an active letters column.

Bowen Islanders responded with enthusiasm. Even though the community was small, people still wanted to know what was going on. The letters column was an immediate hit.

The first issues were mimeographed on a Gestetner machine. It was a daunting task folding and stapling each and every one of those early *Undercurrents*, but Pat Weaver produced regular issues for a year. A supposed brief vacation to the Maritimes turned into a full-time move for Weaver and she sold the paper to Larry Reid.

Reid found the work fascinating and the paper was clearly his. He was a man of strong opinions, and he was not loath to express them. He took stands on gasoline taxes for transit service when he felt Bowen Islanders didn't get any direct benefit. He took very vigorous positions on proposed island development and the decision of local regional district and Islands Trust politicians. He attended community meetings and tracked the work of such bodies as the Advisory Planning Commission and the Islands Trust. But the *Undercurrent* in that period, the 1980s, was probably best known for its letters.

They poured out from Bowen Islanders on all subjects and from all points of view. At times they were vitriolic, at others hilariously funny. Sometimes they were obscure and pointless but mostly they were well targeted and coherent. In the Larry Reid period, the paper went from being a mimeographed newssheet to a lithographed small tabloid. Advertisers and distribution was solicited on the North Shore and its peak circulation almost reached 10,000 copies.

In 1988, Reid sent the word out that he wanted to hang up his editorial pen and publisher's hat. Eric Cardwell, publisher-owner of the Vancouver *West Ender* and *East Ender*, indicated interest. A deal was struck. A new editor and publisher meant a new approach to the *Undercurrent*. Final editorial responsibility was placed in the hands of Agnes Thom, a long-time journalist with the *West Ender*. One of the early decisions was to make the paper weekly.

Changes to editorial policies concerning pseudonyms and libelous material circulated to the Bowen Island community. Subtly, the paper began to change. Letters became less outrageous, a few of the early columnists retired and the paper got a new look. But the need to cover island events and inform Bowen Islanders remained. Attachment to the paper by islanders never ceased.

The paper has since passed from Cardwell to the Metro Valley Newspaper Group. Years of growth and change have characterized the last two decades of Bowen's history and the *Undercurrent*, in a solid, quixotic and, at times, whimsical way, documented it all.

—*Lois Meyers-Carter*

BURNABY AND NEW WESTMINSTER NEWS

The *Burnaby and New Westminster News Leaders* are two of a number of community newspapers that came into being following the demise in the early 1980s of the *Columbian*.

The *News Leaders* began with the name *Sunday News* in mid-1985 and were an integral part of founder Gordy Robson's strategy to

Fiona Combey (publisher) and Greg Knill (editor), Burnaby News Leader, 1998.

blanket the north-east sector of the Lower Mainland with quality, free-distribution, tabloid publications. With the advent of two days of publication each week in 1987, the papers became known as the *News*, and in February of 1996 the name was changed to *News Leader*.

In the fall of 1985 Robson sold his publications to the Metro Valley Group and in December of 1996 David Black, as part of the overall purchase of Trinity International's Canadian division, purchased them. Roy Lind took over publisher responsibilities from Robson, and was later succeeded by Bob Graham, Candy Hodson, Frank Kelly, Brian McCristall and, most recently, Fiona Combey. McCristall retains the title of regional publisher.

First editor of the *Sunday News* was Mark Hamilton and Don Button became editor of the *Burnaby/New West News* in 1987. In 1989 Burnaby and New Westminister editions began to be published. Button, who left the *News* in 1994 to become publisher/editor of the *Fraser Valley Record* (Mission), was at the editorial helm, and Candy Hodson was general manager, when the *News* was named best overall community newspaper in Canada in 1992. Current editor of both *Burnaby* and *New Westminster News Leaders* is Greg Knill.

The *News Leaders* are printed each Wednesday at Van Press and each weekend at Hacker Press while the majority of the composition is completed at the *Tri-City News* production department. All that is quickly changing with the implementation of new technology and more is actually being done on site which enables better service through improved deadlines to readers and advertisers. Today the *News Leaders* strive to maintain high standards in keeping with the suburban markets in which they operate, but the challenge of printing and distributing more than 64,000 copies twice a week is unrelenting. However, members of the editorial staff continue to win provincial and national writing and photography competitions, consistent with past achievements of former staff members Wynn Horn, Claudio D'Andrea, John Wawrow and Guido Marziali.

BURNABY NOW

 The seeds of the *Burnaby Now* began sprouting in the dying days of the *Columbian* daily newspaper in 1983.

The receivers had taken over, circulation was only 30,000 and morale was rock-bottom. But three people saw a chance for a new beginning.

"We started making plans about what we could do if the paper would not survive," recalls Laila Graham, who was then a salesperson. Joined by her husband Neil, the *Columbian's* managing editor, and sales manager Phil Ballard, the group would chat over lunches twice a month. Graham says they discussed equipment, staff, costs and a business plan for creating supplement weeklies. "We even looked at some office space in New Westminster."

When the receivers announced the *Columbian* would end its 123 years of operation Tuesday Nov. 15, 1983, the three immediately put in a bid to get the rights to the name *Today*. So did *Columbian* owner Rikk Taylor.

The supplement weeklies, with a combined circulation of 160,000, were capable of making money. But Taylor submitted the high bid and walked away with the name.

While the Lower Mainland media focused on chronicling the demise of the *Columbian*, the three decided to try and publish a paper in Burnaby the very next week.

"It was approaching Christmas at that time. I had about $5,000 worth of advertising business in hand and I was not about to let it go. We knew the only way we could survive was if we didn't miss one publication," Graham remembers.

A group of former *Columbian* employees joined the venture, each contributing $10,000 as operating money, adopting the corporate name of Courage Inc. The *Now* in the masthead was an idea thought up by Laila Graham since the rights of *Today* sat in Taylor's hands. The first edition of the *Burnaby Now* was a 12-page broadsheet with some 40,000 copies distributed. The next two subsequent issues were 10 and 12 pages respectively.

The original investment group began casting for additional capital and found a partner in Lower Mainland Publishing Ltd., which purchased a 50 per cent share in the company.

From that point on, the *Burnaby Now* was a growing suburban weekly group of *Now* newspapers that would eventually include New Westminster, Surrey and Coquitlam.

The new company continued to struggle with its future still in doubt when it received a major economic shot in the arm. The two Vancouver daily newspapers, the *Province* and *Vancouver Sun*, went on strike allowing all the *Now* papers to establish an advertising and readership foothold in their communities. In the years since then, the *Burnaby Now* switched to a tabloid format and began publishing twice a week, Sundays and Wednesdays.

There have been ownership changes since the early days: the original investors were eventually bought out by LMPL, which in turn sold a majority interest of the company to Southam.

Chilliwack Progress

C.E.C. Hacker first came to Chilliwack in 1931 to do research for an essay on missionaries that he was completing at the University of British Columbia.

In 1933, Charles Barber offered him a job selling advertising at the *Progress*.

Hacker took the job but then left the paper for three years, returning in 1939.

After the Second World War, Les Barber, D'arcy Baldwin and

Julian Galbecka, current publisher of the Progress, 1998.

Hacker arranged to lease the paper from Charles Barber. When Baldwin's career took him elsewhere, Les wanted ownership of the family newspaper so the partnership dissolved with Hacker purchasing the *Abbotsford News*.

In 1962, when the Liverpool Post and Echo Limited purchased the *Progress*, the *ASM News* and the *Fraser Valley Record*, Hacker was appointed publisher.

A former advertising manager with the *Progress*, Roy Lind was appointed publisher on Hacker's retirement in 1978.

Lind was born in Abbotsford, getting his start in newspapers in the circulation department of a Vancouver daily.

He took a position in advertising sales at the *Abbotsford News* in 1967, moving to Chilliwack as ad sales manager in 1968. Lind held that position until 1973 when he became business manager, holding that post until his promotion to publisher.

At the same time, in 1978, Liverpool acquired the *Hope Standard* and Lind was named publisher of both papers.

Notable changes at the *Progress* during Lind's publishership included the purchase, development and move to the current Spadina Avenue property in 1974, and the conversion from hot metal to computerized typesetting. Lind also shepherded the change from typewriters to computers in both the editorial and classified ad departments.

In 1985 Lind left the *Progress* to become publisher of the *Maple Ridge News*, *Tri-City News* and *Sunday News* (North Burnaby) when those papers were purchased by Liverpool. In 1988, Lind took the position of vice-president of marketing for the Metro Valley Newspaper Group (Trinity's marketing arm in the Fraser Valley). Jim

The Chilliwack Progress, *1998.*

Robertson, a former reporter and editor of the *Progress*, was appointed publisher on Lind's departure in 1985.

Robertson, who had worked for CBC radio and television in Montreal and Toronto, moved to Abbotsford in 1975. He started at the *Progress* in 1978 as a reporter covering community news, business and agriculture. He became the editor of the paper in 1980, and held that position for five years until he became publisher.

As editor, Robertson particularly enjoyed the hotline to the editor, an hour and a half every Thursday morning when he answered telephone calls from readers — sometimes acting as an ombudsman, sometimes as information source.

As publisher, Robertson was "very proud of the staff of the *Progress* and the way they pulled together in maintaining a newspaper of very high integrity."

Robertson left the *Progress* to join his wife in their family's graphics company. He now specializes in computer systems consultations throughout the province.

On Robertson's departure in 1990, the duties of Randy Blair, publisher of the *Progress'* sister papers the *Abbotsford News* and the *Fraser Valley Record*, expanded to include both the *Progress* and the *Hope Standard*. Blair had been publisher of the *News* and the *Record* since 1989. He started his newspaper career 22 years ago in advertising sales with the Reliance Press in Winnipeg. His last position before

Don Campbell (Salmon Arm), Bart Creighton (Duncan), Lang Sands (Abbotsford), Grev Rowland (Penticton), Edgar Dunning (Ladner), Fred Bass (CKWX), Roy McLean (Kelowna) and Hugh McIntyre (Sidney) at the Hotel Vancouver, 1942.

joining the Metro Valley Group was at Southam Newspapers in Winnipeg. He worked as advertising manager of both Flyer Force and four weekly suburban newspapers for Southam.

In 1933, Julian Galbecka was appointed publisher of the *Progress*. Galbecka came from Winnipeg, where he was running his own commercial printing business. Prior to that he had worked with the *Winnipeg Free Press* for six years in advertising sales, and had spent 12 years with Canadian Publishers Ltd. in the web printing industry.

"I was impressed with the newspaper because of its quality, and the community of Chilliwack," says Galbecka.

During this time, the *Progress* went through some significant changes, including the installation of Macintosh computers in 1994, which allowed compositors and editorial staff new freedom in production of news pages and advertising.

In 1996, the traditional Wednesday publication date of the midweek *Progress* was changed to Tuesday in order to better serve the local market. In February 1998, the *Progress* added a Sunday edition to its lineup, turning the paper for the first time into a three-times-a-week publication. The creation of an on-line edition of the *Progress* on the Internet in 1997 was a first for the Metro Valley Newspaper Group.

A broader change was the 1997 purchase of Metro Valley by B.C.'s David Black of Black Press. The purchase brings B.C. ownership back to the paper after 35 years of British control.

"I think we'll be more and more dependent on technology to produce papers," Galbecka says. "In the time I've been here we've added some annual, quarterly publications and I think that's what we'll continue doing . . . "

COQUITLAM/ PORT COQUITLAM/ PORT MOODY/ ANMORE/ BELCARRA NOW

1983 and 1984 was a busy time for the *Now* newspaper expansion. The *Coquitlam Now, Port Coquitlam, Port Moody, Anmore, Belcarra Now* began production in January 1984, in conjunction with the *Surrey Now* and *New Westminster Now*.

Offices were filled with familiar faces because many of the staff had worked for the *Columbian* or its group of weeklies; sadly, those papers had gone into receivership in the fall of 1983. The *Columbian's* loss was the *Now* newspapers' gain.

The *Now* paper started as a once-a-week broadsheet in the worst business month of the year — January. The paper struggled like all new business ventures until March of 1984. That's when the two major dailies, the *Vancouver Sun* and the *Province*, went out on a long strike and major advertisers started calling. The *Now* was on the map.

COQUITLAM/ PORT COQUITLAM/ PORT MOODY TRI-CITY NEWS

The *Tri-City News* is one of a number of thriving community newspaper publications which came into being following the demise in the early 1980s of the *Columbian, Coquitlam Enterprise, Port Coquitlam Herald* and *Today* newspapers.

The *Tri-City News*, which serves the burgeoning communities of

Brian McCristall and Roy Lind, 1998.

Coquitlam, Port Coquitlam, Port Moody and the villages of Belcarra and Anmore, was first established by Gordy Robson in May of 1985 and was purchased by Metro Valley in November of that year. It was subsequently sold to David Black in December of 1996, as part of his overall purchase of Trinity International's Canadian division.

The *News* has been tabloid in format and distributed free of charge since its inception. Initially it published once a week, but after being purchased by Metro Valley its frequency was soon increased to twice a week. Per-issue distribution has grown from about 30,000 to more than 50,000 as of 1998.

First launched from the Maple Ridge office, the *News* soon moved to premises on Clarke Road, on the Coquitlam/Burnaby border. It continued to be composed in Maple Ridge and printed in Abbotsford at Hacker Press. However, in 1989 it relocated to new and enlarged premises at 1405 Broadway in Port Coquitlam. The offices house central composing, bindery, circulation and administration functions for sister *News/News Leader* publications in Maple Ridge/ Pitt Meadows, Burnaby and New Westminster. Seventy-five full-time staff work out of that location. Presswork is still done at Hacker Press in Abbotsford.

Photo by Craig Hodge, Tri-City News.

Also located in the same facility is the B.C. Newspaper Group, which is headed by Roy Lind, who was a driving force during the *News'* formative years.

From the outset, the *Tri-City News* has been recognized as a community leader in news and photo coverage and was among the first community newspapers to adopt a full-colour format on a regular basis.

Photo by Mario Bartel, Coquitlam Tri-City News.

Photo by Eike Schroeder, Tri-City News.

The first editor was Mark Hamilton. He held that post for 12 years before resigning in 1997 to start his own graphics design company. During Hamilton's tenure at the *News* it won a variety of reporting, writing and general excellence awards provincially and nationally. Diane Strandberg was appointed editor in July of 1997.

Chief photographer is Craig Hodge, who has been with the company since its inception.

Today, the *Tri-City News* maintains high standards and continues to be the community leader in the very complex and challenging job of "getting the news out" to diversified, growing communities.

"There has been a great deal of change in community newspapers in the past decade and much of that has been forced upon the business as a direct result of reader, advertiser and market demands," says Brian McCristall, the paper's current publisher.

What does the future hold?

"More success, I hope," McCristall says, "but it won't be achieved without continuing to strive for excellence. Ultimately, our success is inextricably linked to our ability to serve our readers, our advertisers and our communities. As everyone knows, change is the constant that enables that high level of service to be provided."

DELTA OPTIMIST

The first weekly newspaper to be established to serve Ladner and district was the *Delta Times*, which began publication in 1903. Its managing director was J.D. Taylor and it was produced by the *Columbian*, of New Westminster.

There was reputed to be a population of 1,000 at that time and the paper turned out 500 copies. Its size was six columns by 20 inches and was generally of eight pages. No information is available on how long this paper continued to publish.

In March 1922 V.C. Dunning and his wife Gertrude came to the Delta district and established the *Ladner Optimist*. Population around this period was estimated at 2,500 in the municipality. An association rate card published in 1931 stated the circulation figures were about 750.

The Dunnings had three sons who learned the trade while they produced the weekly newspaper and on their passing the boys took command of the business and kept it going. Over the years both Edgar and Eric Dunning were prominent in the provincial and national newspaper organizations and both served as president of the B.C. Weekly Newspapers Association.

Eric left the home weekly to establish his own paper in Haney, continuing as its publisher until his sudden passing in 1971. Edgar was joined in the publication of the *Ladner Optimist* in 1963 by E.G. (Ernie) Bexley, who acquired a half interest in Dunning

Tom Siba (Delta Optimist) *and Manfred Tempelmayr* (Duncan/Cowichan Pictorial).

Photo by Brian Langdeau, Coquitlam Tri-City News.

Press Ltd. A former advertising manager for the *Surrey Leader*, he went on to become co-publisher and advertising manager of the *Optimist* in Ladner, eventually purchasing the entire operation in 1974.

Bexley saw the *Optimist* grow along with the expansion of the Delta District. In 1990, the Bexley family sold the *Optimist* to Southam Newspapers, which rolled it into the newly formed Lower Mainland Publishing Ltd.. At the same time, Lower Mainland Publishing acquired the weekly *South Delta Today*, which had been publishing since 1989 in Ladner and Tsawwassen.

In 1991, Tom Siba, the publisher of *South Delta Today*, was appointed publisher of the *Optimist* and the two paper were merged into a three times a week publication. The following year, the North Delta edition of the *Optimist* was combined into the *Surrey/North Delta Now*, another member of the LMPL family. In 1995, the *Optimist* changed to two issues a week—Wednesday and Saturday—and continues to serve its loyal readers in the region.

GIBSONS, THE COAST INDEPENDENT

The *Coast Independent* is the oldest and best-read paper serving the Sunshine Coast of B.C., a short ferry ride from Horseshoe Bay in West Vancouver.

The *Independent* carries on the proud tradition of the *Sunshine Coast News*, which was closed by its owners in January of 1995 after 50 straight years of covering the area.

Two weeks later, a small group of former Coast News employees, with the moral and financial support of hundreds of readers from up and down the coast, launched the first issue of the *Coast Independent* out of a closet-sized office above a convenience store in the heart of Gibsons.

Since that time, the paper has blossomed from a sparse, 12-page broadsheet, into a bi-weekly tabloid format averaging 60 pages a week, and the grotty little office above a convenience store has

B.C. Division, CWNA, 32nd Annual Meeting, Hotel Vancouver, Sept. 20-23, 1950

evolved into two full-fledged and fairly respectable offices in both Gibsons and Sechelt.

The *Independent* is owned and operated by a core group of five people: Jane Seyd and Darah Hansen, editors and writers extraordinaire; Sue Connor, publisher and accounting guru; Andy Jukes, production manager and trivia king; and Joel Johnstone, photographer, visionary and Mr. Fix-It. All are supported by an enthusiastic and talented team of about a dozen sales staff, writers, graphic designers and office personnel.

The five-way ownership has been an enlightening and at times trying experience, but through it all the team has learned a lot about the business principles that carried them past the "Hey! Let's start a paper!" phase and into producing a viable, economically-sound independent news product.

"We take a great deal of pride in the fact that we are a truly independent newspaper in an age when such a beast is an increasing rarity," say the owners. "And that we are staffed by people who know and care about the communities they live in.

"The Sunshine Coast is a unique and wonderful place to live and we feel both proud and privileged to participate in the creation of the 'newspaper of record' for our area. We look forward to serving our readers with a commitment to quality for many years to come."

HOPE STANDARD

The first newspaper published in the Hope district, *British Columbia Tribune*, was established at nearby Yale in 1866. This was the work of George Wallace who had launched the *Cariboo Sentinel* in 1965.

The *Tribune* was followed by the *British Columbia Examiner* in 1868, also at Yale. This paper lasted for only about a year.

Michael Hagan started the *Inland Sentinel* in 1880 at Emory Creek. Only a few issues were published at Emory Creek. The plant and office were moved to Yale, where it was published until 1884. Soon after, the entire operation moved to Kamloops and Hope was without a local paper.

In 1910, during the excitement of the Steamboat Mountain gold rush, two papers were started at Hope — the *Gold Trail* and the *Steamboat Nugget*. They later amalgamated as the *Hope News* and the *Gold Trail*. This venture was short-lived.

The next paper was the *West Yale Review*, published in 1910 with J. Dennie as publisher and George Clark as editor. The plant was located on First Avenue near Wallace Street in Hope.

The *Hope News* was started in 1923 with J. Juniur Dougan as editor and Edward Hagell as manager. The *Hope-Agassiz-Harrison News* started publishing on March 18, 1938, but only lasted for a short time.

The *Hope and District Chronicle* was printed at Hope by the Chronicle Publishing Ltd. on January 5, 1950. Forerunner to the present *Hope Standard*, it was established by Ed Shirton and he continued until 1952 when he sold it to J.B. Creighton, a former managing editor of the *Cowichan Leader*.

Today the *Hope Standard* is a part of the Metro Valley Newspaper Group, which includes sister papers *Abbotsford News* and *Chilliwack Progress*.

Jim Schatz (Langley Advance) presented this New Zealand book to President Ernie Bexley (Delta Optimist). The book had been given to the B.C. Community papers by Frank Smedden, the New Zealand publisher who visited B.C. in 1971.

LANGLEY ADVANCE NEWS

The *Langley Advance News*, initially entitled the *Langley Advance*, hit Langley's streets for the first time on July 23, 1931. By the end of the 1930s it had become Langley's premier source for community news and information.

Langley's most comprehensive news coverage had been provided up to that time by the weekly *New Westminster Columbian* through a network of local correspondents.

Other than the *Columbian*, Langley got its first local newspaper on March 22, 1911. The *Langley Leader*, published by R.G. Dingle and edited by R.D. Clarke, was printed in New Westminster, with a local office in Fort Langley. The needs of Langley at that time were listed as a good drug store, a barbershop and something in the line of evening entertainment. The four-page tab's first edition featured a photograph of Langley's 1910 district agriculture exhibit, which had placed second in the New Westminster Exhibition.

How long the *Langley Leader* lasted is not recorded. It was started at a time when local commerce via steamboat to New Westminster was on the verge of being replaced by rail service, and by the B.C. Electric Interurban passenger line connecting Chilliwack and New Westminster.

By the time the *Valley Sentinel* appeared in Langley in 1921, the *Leader* was out of the scene. Little is known about the *Sentinel*, except that it did not last long.

The next publishing effort in Langley was undertaken by the Langley Board of Trade, which sponsored a tabloid called the *Langley Lantern*. There were three issues, published on November 8 and December 15, 1922, and January 10, 1923. It was produced by editor Ivan Hurndall, news editor E. Streatfield and advertising manager N.C. Abercrombie.

G.Y. Timms, a businessman who founded Langley Greenhouses, operated a print shop in New Westminster, and built a number of Langley's first business blocks. He founded the *Langley Press* in 1925 and kept it going for about a year. On May 7, 1925, the *Press* reported that between 4,000 and 5,000 people attended a centenary celebration in Fort Langley, representing just about the total population of

Photo by Doug Shanks.

the area, and three motorists had been fined for exceeding the speed limit in town.

From mid-1926 to August 1931, the *Columbian* newspaper had Langley all to itself.

Early in 1931, Ernest J. Cox sold his interests in a North Battleford, Saskatchewan, shop and moved to B.C. to take a half interest with Gerald Heller in the Abbotsford News. At the same time, the Langley Board of Trade had been negotiating with Heller to set up a new paper in Langley Prairie (now Langley City). Cox undertook the task of getting the Langley Advance started, and the first issue, six columns on four pages printed in Abbotsford and four pages of boiler plate, came out on July 23, 1931. Since that date, the Advance (now the Langley Advance News) has not missed a single week of publication.

A few months after the *Advance* was founded, the partnership between Cox and Heller was dissolved with Cox retaining the *Advance* and Heller staying in Abbotsford.

Assisting Cox in getting the *Advance* under way were his wife and their two teenaged children, Fred and Kathleen. In spite of the hard times of the depression, the *Advance* grew as the Langley area steadily developed. The war years were also difficult, with young Fred leaving to join the armed forces.

After the war, Fred Cox returned to the *Advance*, along with George Johnson, an RAF instructor in the Empire Air Training Program, who had married Kathleen. The next year, 1947, Jim Schatz joined the staff.

In 1948 the *Advance* founded a paper in Aldergrove, a satellite community to the east. The *Optimist* lasted nearly four years before the effort was abandoned.

In the meantime, The Langley Advance Publishing Co. Ltd. was formed in 1949 with the principals being E.J. and Fred Cox, Johnson and Schatz. At the same time three fellows from Powell River started an opposition newspaper, the *Langley Times*, which had a stormy history, including an abortive attempt as a Fraser Valley-wide daily, before it succumbed in 1953.

In 1958 E.J. Cox went into semi-retirement and Fred Cox sold his interests in the company, but purchased the commercial printing portion of the business.

Johnson and Schatz remained as the principals in the *Advance* until the end of the 1970s when Rod Sharp took on that position.

During this period, the *Advance* found itself in competition with one of its own employees, Jack Dunham, who left his position as production manager to start his own newspaper, the *Fraser Valley News Herald*. The *Herald* offered stiff competition for a few years, but went into decline and was out of the picture by the time another upstart, the *Local News*, appeared in Langley. The latter publication was short-lived, however, and the field was once again the *Advance's* alone, until a new *Langley Times* came on the scene in 1981.

Schatz, acting as both publisher and editor of the *Advance* during this period, as well as sole owner, was involved with the British Columbia and Yukon Community Newspapers Association and the

Canadian Community Newspapers Association, serving as president of the BCYCNA in 1970-71 and of the CCNA in 1980-81.

Bob Groeneveld, who started with the paper as a reporter in 1977, became news editor in 1981 and remains at the *Langley Advance News* as editor today.

Jim Schatz died suddenly on February 4, 1990. His wife Norma took over as the publisher and his son Ian became general manager, running most of the business's day-to-day affairs. A changing business climate and competition from a new *Langley Times*, which started as an independent in 1981 and later was taken over by an international chain of newspapers, sent the *Langley Advance* into financial decline which ended with its sale to Marilyn Boswyk on September 14, 1994.

Until its decline in the late 1980s, the *Advance* had a reputation as a pioneer in weekly newspapers. In 1947 the *Advance* was one of the first shops outside a metropolitan area to install a modern multilith. A short while later the first Klischograph engraver to be installed in western Canada was purchased by the *Advance*, in response to a beginning trend toward greater pictorial emphasis. It was in the engraving department of the *Advance* that it was first discovered that black and white engravings could be made directly on the engraver by simply using the reverse setting. The *Advance* went to offset printing in 1968, and a year later a Justowriter system was installed to set cold-type copy for the news columns. Full conversion to offset was attained in 1971 with the installation of a Friden photo-typesetting headliner. In 1980 the *Advance* installed a state-of-the art Linotype computer system, with a refrigerator-sized mainframe and half a dozen slave terminals. Although the best of its kind in its day, the hundreds of thousands of dollars worth of equipment had about a fifth of the memory storage and only a tiny fraction of the capabilities of just one of today's desktop computer stations.

Among Boswyk's first moves as the *Advance's* new publisher was to bring the operation back up to speed technologically, installing new computer equipment and aligning the newspaper, still an independently owned organ, with the Southam-dominated VanNet newspapers operated throughout the Fraser Valley. In the late 1980s, a weekend-tab, free-circulation "advertiser" had been revamped into a second edition to the mid-week broadsheet. The broadsheet was

Photo by Rob Newell, Langley Times.

later published as a tab, but remained available by subscription. Boswyk changed both editions to blanket distribution and bumped their circulation to bring the *Advance* into all Langley homes. Ryc Fowler was brought in as advertising manager, and *News* was added to the *Advance's* name to re-assert the paper's emphasis on community news and information.

LANGLEY TIMES

The *Langley Times* began as a family business under publisher Gerry Maginn. The first paper was published on February 18, 1981 from a second-floor office on 56th Avenue in downtown Langley City. In 1983, the *Times* was voted in as a member of the B.C. and Yukon Community Newspapers Association and the Canadian Community Newspapers Association.

By 1984, the paper had moved onto Langley's main street — Fraser Highway — converting the former Toronto-Dominion Bank building into a newspaper facility. The darkroom was, fittingly enough, in what used to be the vault.

In 1985 the paper increased its frequency to twice each week. The *Times* was purchased in 1986 by the Metro Valley Newspaper Group, which included papers like the *Abbotsford News* and *Surrey/North Delta Leader*.

Tanis Culley, the former advertising manager of the *Times*, became publisher in 1991.

The *Times* is distributed in the east Surrey/Langley area from Cloverdale to Aldergrove. The *Times* moved to a new office at 20258 Fraser Highway in 1995 but remained in downtown Langley.

LILLOOET NEWS

This year (1998) marks 64 years of publication of the *Bridge River-Lillooet News*, a newspaper made famous by its founding publisher and editor, Margaret Lally "Ma" Murray.

The flag on page two of Ma's paper always read: "Printed in the sage brush country of the Lillooet every Thursday, God willing.

Bob Berman, 1996

Guarantees a chuckle every week and a belly laugh once a month or your money back. Subscriptions $5.00 in Canada. Furriners $6.00. This week's circulation 1,726 and every bloody one of them paid for." That gives you an inkling of the kind of homespun homilies and common-sense commentary that filled its pages. But it was Ma's dauntless courage in the pursuit of the betterment of her community that really made her an icon not only in Lillooet, but also across British Columbia.

Born in Windy Ridge, Kansas, in 1887, Ma arrived in Lillooet in 1933 after her husband, George Matheson Murray, an eminent newspaperman in Vancouver, won the seat for the Liberals in the provincial election. One of George Murray's election promises was to establish a newspaper in the community and Volume 1, No. 1 of the *News* rolled off the presses on Thursday, March 1, 1934.

Ma quickly became famous, turning out a weekly broadsheet that portrayed the life and times of Lillooet and the political scene further abroad with equal candor. She wrote the stories and filled the newspaper without fail, operating in 1940s wartime with an all-female staff of three. Ma ran the *Bridge River-Lillooet News* for eight years while her husband lobbied for the railway extension and improved roads to the Bridge River gold mines, negotiated tax breaks for ranchers and wage settlements with striking miners and promoted higher education standards for the province's youth.

When George failed to regain his seat in 1942 he turned his energies north to the Peace River country and Fort St. John. Ma put the *Bridge River-Lillooet News* on the back burner and joined him, starting up the *Alaska Highway News*. Both the *Alaska Highway News* and the *Lillooet News* were shipped out to Vancouver for printing. When a water shortage hit Fort St. John in the 1950s, Ma penned an appropriate editorial:

". . . To head off this catastrophe, only flush for No. 2, curtail bathing to the Saturday night tub, go back to the washrag, which could always move a lot of B.O. if applied often enough."

Water consumption in Fort St. John dropped 65,000 gallons daily. Through the editorial efforts of the *Alaska Highway News* and George's hard lobbying, the railway made it to Fort St. John in 1958. Following the realization of George's dream, the couple decided to semi-retire in Lillooet in 1961 but tragedy struck before their plans could mature. On his way back to Lillooet George had an automobile accident and died from his injuries soon after, leaving Ma to run the *Bridge River-Lillooet News* alone.

Her salty wit, forthright dealings with politicians and courageous commentary in the face of numerous controversies earned Ma the respect of politicians across the province. She appeared on *Front Page Challenge*, in *Time Magazine* and on various radio talk shows, always blunt, always honest and always full of vibrant life.

Ma spent the next 10 years chastising elected officials, dispensing her hard-earned wisdom in healthy doses and becoming a living legend in the journalistic field.

She lived on the upper floor of the news office where she and George first started the *Bridge River-Lillooet News* in 1934. The old building still stands at 545 Main Street, now converted to private apartments. In 1973, Ma Murray sold the *Bridge River-Lillooet News* to Dutch printer Jeff den Biesen, who carried on the paper's tradition of fine community journalism. Over the next 20 years den Biesen developed his own reputation as a journalist who never shied away from controversy and as a great advocate for his community.

B.C. Hydro lunch, October 1976. Left to right: Jim McCarthy (B.C. Hydro), Ernie Bexley (Delta Optimist), Chuck MacLean (then CCNA president, Camrose, Alberta), Robert Bonner (then Chair of B.C. Hydro).

Jeff den Biesen was also an active member of newspaper associations on a provincial, regional and national level. In 1991, the newspaper was purchased by Whistler Printing and Publishing, a division of the company that became WestMount Press Ltd. When Ontario-based Bowes Publishers purchased WestMount in the spring of 1998, the *Bridge River-Lillooet News* was part of the deal, but Bowes Publishers sold its interest in the paper to Lower Mainland Publishing of Vancouver in July of 1998.

Margaret Lally Murray passed away quietly on September 25, 1982, at the age of 94 surrounded by her family, in her old suite above the news office. Her body was taken to Fort St. John, where she was laid to rest beside her beloved husband, George.

Ma's legacy remains, not only in Lillooet, but also in the journalism profession. More than one university includes a section on Ma Murray in its curriculum. She is remembered for her integrity and for her colourful turn of phrase — and that's for damshur!

Photo by C.J. Relke, Maple Ridge-Pitt Meadows Times.

MAPLE RIDGE/ PITT MEADOWS NEWS

With very little fanfare and not even capital letters in its name-plate, the very first *Maple Ridge-Pitt Meadows News* arrived from Langley via the Albion Ferry on February 1, 1978—called simply *the local news*.

Its front page carried a political story about the selection of "ruggedly good-looking" Coquitlam lawyer Tom Spraggs as the Liberal candidate for the federal riding of Mission-Port Moody.

The *local news*, one of the early free-distribution papers to take on established weeklies like the *Gazette* in Maple Ridge, was a spin-off of a Langley publication associated with movie theatres operating on both sides of the Fraser River.

Its early editions were heavy on promotional materials for the hottest current films, such as Saturday Night Fever and its emerging star, John Travolta.

In its fourth month of publication, an angry front page "declaration of independence" described the end of Langley rule, next to a story about the closing of the movie theatres in both Maple Ridge and Langley. Advertising representative Robert Long announced he was the new owner-publisher and that "an impossible situation has been rectified."

"At *the local news* editorial content was dictated by insufficient time and confusion," says Long.

Two decades later there have been numerous changes in ownership and technology, staff claim they are still working on that "insufficient time" problem.

Long later sold the *News* to another local resident, Gordon Robson, who in turn sold it in 1985 to Trinity International plc, a British newspaper company that assembled the Metro Valley Newspaper Group, joining community newspapers from Hope to Vancouver around press facilities in Abbotsford.

In 1997 Victoria businessman David Black purchased the Metro Valley Group, adding it to his Island Publishers and Cariboo Press groups of community papers.

The face of the *News* has gone through a few changes over the years. One of those was the *Sunday News*, a feature-oriented regional

Photo by Simone Ponne, Maple Ridge-Pitt Meadows News.

publication that served to extend the *News'* distribution system westward to Coquitlam and Burnaby. Under the direction of publisher Roy Lind and managing editor Frank Klassen, the groundwork was laid to turn the *News* into a thriving twice-weekly and launch its successful sister papers, the *Tri City News*, the *Burnaby News Leader* and the *New Westminster News Leader*.

When it came to technology, Klassen saw to it that the *News* was an "early adopter" as they say. When the new-fangled Macintosh computer was introduced, this was one of the first places it went to work, and it was the development of desktop publishing equipment and modern links that sped the expansion of the *News* from Maple Ridge westward.

Since 1990, the *Sunday News* has been transformed into a full-service community newspaper in each of the communities it serves. Along the way, the *News* staff like to think the Metro Valley Newspaper Group helped raise the journalistic standard for community newspapers in the province and the country and continues to provide a service in exchange for a place on the reader's porch.

MISSION CITY RECORD

The late J.A. Bates founded the *Mission City Record* in 1908. Called the *Fraser Valley Record* until 1996, the paper was renamed to carry the name of the principal community it served. Although launched with grand plans of expanding coverage to include the entire Fraser Valley, the *Record* has always been the community newspaper for Mission, B.C.. Mission City was the original name of Mission and the name continues to be used. To honour the history of the community and the paper, the *Record* chose Mission City over Mission for its new name.

The paper's first office was a building measuring about 12 by 12 feet in the bush near the CPR right-of-way near Horne Street. As the town grew, larger premises were erected on Main Street, followed later by a further extension of 60 feet.

Initially the *Record* was handset. It was among the earliest to install the largest Linotype made and even this had to be augmented with a Ludlow typecasting machine. Several new presses served the *Record* over the years. In the 1940s, a two-page press was used and the paper was hand-folded.

By 1951, a four-page press had been installed with a folding machine, greatly speeding up production. Newspaper sections still had to be stuffed by hand. In 1956, the *Record* installed its own electronic engraving machine, making plastic cuts from photographs and copy.

When Bates founded the *Record*, he intended it to serve the communities of Agassiz, Harrison, Harrison Mills, Hatzic, Mission City, Matsqui, Abbotsford, Langley, Haney, Hammond, Coquitlam, Port Moody and surrounding districts. The *Record* now serves Mission, Hatzic and Harrison Mills from the preceeding list, plus Dewdney, Deroche, Silverdale, Ruskin, McConnell Creek, Stave Lake/Falls, Lake Errock and Hemlock Valley.

Although Bates did not achieve his territory goals for the *Record*, he did establish another paper on the south side of the Fraser: the *Abbotsford Post*, in which the *Abbotsford News* has its roots.

In its 90 years of existence, the *Record* has had five owners. The first three owners were individuals: J.A. Bates, R.D. Cumming of Ashcroft and Lang Sands, who was owner of the *Abbotsford, Sumas* and *Matsqui News* when he took over the *Record* in July 1944. The paper was purchased in 1962 by the Liverpool Daily Post and Echo Holdings (Trinity International), which developed the Metro Valley Group of community newspapers in Greater Vancouver. David Black, publisher of over 50 community newspapers, purchased the Metro Valley Group, including the *Record*, at the end of 1996.

During the 1920s and early 1930s, the *Record* was leased to B. Stone Kennedy of New Westminster, and at the time of its sale to Sands, was published by Lew Cumming on behalf of his father, a publisher in Ashcroft.

Soon after Lang Sands took over the *Record* in 1944, Kenneth Plowright, who bought an interest and became a working partner, joined him. That relationship lasted until 1950, when Plowright left.

In 1964, the *Record* was the first weekly newspaper in the Central Fraser Valley to be produced on a high-speed offset newspaper press at the *Abbotsford News* plant.

John Evans, who retired to Mission, managed the *Record* for over two decades.

Current publisher and editor is Don Button, who joined the *Record* in 1993 from the *Burnaby News* in the Metro Valley Group.

NEW WESTMINSTER, ROYAL CITY RECORD

 What do you need when starting a community newspaper? A kitchen table and the trunk of a car.

That's all Ron Loftus used for those first few editions of a small newspaper he started 17 years ago which became the talk of the town — and still is. Loftus was a long-time New Westminster resident who believed the heart of his city had been forgotten by its newspaper.

The *Columbian* newspaper, one of the first newspapers in B.C., was founded in 1861 as the *British Columbian*. It was New Westminster's voice. But by the 1970s it was waning and had lost its community focus. Loftus could see an opportunity. He'd worked at the *Columbian* for seven years — hired straight out of high school — and then at the *Vancouver Sun* for 20 years.

His newspaper sense said New Westminster needed its own voice.

Photo by Arlen Redekop, New Westminster News Leader.

Loftus talked a half dozen of his friends into kicking in a few dollars each to get the infant paper off the ground, which they did October 1, 1981. But what a challenge.

The first issue, written mainly by Loftus and former *Columbian* reporter Adelle Jack, was to be typeset locally. But after a day of work, the typesetter disappeared, and Loftus, stuck with raw copy and a deadline looming, bundled the copy up and flew it to friend Rollie Rose (another *Columbian* "grad" and former New Westminster boy) in Ladysmith. There it was typeset and printed by Island Publishers.

The Loftus family packed that first issue into the trunk of their car and delivered it themselves — with the help of a few friends — door to door across the city. It took them a week.

Photo by Neil Lucente, North Shore News.

"Delivering 22,000 papers in New Westminster was no picnic with all those damn hills," says Loftus with a smile.

Readers quickly embraced the paper as their hometown newspaper.

A few years later, the *Columbian* closed its doors and the *Record* was in direct competition with the *Now* newspapers, launched on the heels of the *Columbian's* demise.

More money was injected into the *Royal City Record* when Steven Houston bought half of it. Homegrown it was, but because New Westminster was such a tiny market in the large metropolis of Vancouver, the independent *Royal City Record* couldn't compete with the chain newspapers which attracted the large, national advertisers.

Eventually it would have to strike a deal, which Houston did, selling it to the *Now* chain.

Today the *Royal City Record* is known as the *Record* and retains its position as the city's hometown newspaper.

Why did Loftus call it the *Royal City Record?*

"When I was a little kid there was a paper called the *Royal City Record*. It only showed up whenever they sold enough ads or felt like printing it. But I loved it because it ran our soccer scores."

NORTH VANCOUVER, NORTH SHORE NEWS

The *North Shore News* rose like a phoenix out of the ashes of a long-standing battle for North Shore newspaper supremacy.

The history goes like this: In the area's early days there was only one newspaper, the *North Shore Press*. In 1926, a challenge to the territory began with the *Review*, later called the *North Shore Review*. Then in the late '30s, a printer, James Towgood, started the *Lions Gate Times* to try to capture the growing West Vancouver population.

In 1955, *Review* owner J.M. Bryan, reporter Ralph Hall and advertising manager Welly Boyes decided to buy the *Press*. They kept both weeklies running until 1957 when they merged the two into the *North Shore Press Review*. When long-time and well-known newspaperman H.L. "Hal" Straight came on the scene in 1958, he bought the *Press-Review* and changed its name to the *Citizen*.

Peter Speck entered the fray in the late '60s and although he probably dreamed about it, he didn't set out to take on the three existing papers. Speck started out selling ads for the *Lions Gate Times*, by 1968 a weekly West Vancouver paper published by Claude Hoodspith. When Speck broached Hoodspith with the idea

Peter Speck, publisher of the North Shore News, 1998.

NORTH SHORE SHOPPER for DECEMBER

North Van is home to famous
COAD CANADA PUPPETS

COMING EVENTS

of a free flyer to be distributed by the *Times* to every house on the North Shore from Deep Cove to Horseshoe Bay, the idea wasn't exactly jumped at.

So in 1969 he went out on his own. With "50 cents in my pockets and holes in my shoes" Speck began a once-a-week flyer called the *North Shore Shopper* with no editorial content.

It started with a circulation of 6,000. By 1977 it had a new name, the *North Shore News*, and a circulation of 46,000. The flyer had become a full-fledged newspaper with three editorial staff, including editor-in-chief Noel Wright.

Speck's newspaper covered the news in a more sensational way than the other more staid North Shore publications. On the front page would be a murder case or a gruesome car wreck as opposed to perhaps news of city council meetings on the front page of the rival papers. As an example, on the front page of the June 1, 1977, *News*, the banner headline was of a married couple busted for drugs, a police crackdown on illegal booze possession and a wild, 80-mph police chase.

On the *Citizen's* front page was a banner story about a fired city clerk and development plans for Deep Cove.

"We have a bright, lively colourful format and touch on subjects they don't," said Speck in a 1977 interview with the *Vancouver Sun*. At the time he also attributed his success to free ads for seniors and community groups and his tabloid format and efficient delivery system.

The *News* has also traditionally featured controversial and outspoken columnists such as Doug Collins, Bob Hunter, Trevor Lautens and the late Les Bewley.

A year after Speck roared on to the scene, the *Lions Gate Times* shut down after publishing for 30 years. Hoodspith put up a valiant fight and even had expanded his paper to cover the entire North Shore — but finally just couldn't compete with the more provocative, colourful and free, total-market-coverage *North Shore News*.

The *News* continued to grow. A Sunday edition was added to the original Wednesday *News* in April 1977 and a Friday edition was added in February 1984. Competitors for the North Shore community newspaper crown continued to take runs at the *News*, but Speck's publication turned back all challengers and continues to do so. To date, at least 40 competing publications have been dispatched by the *News*.

Speck sold the newspaper to Southam in 1989 to devote more time to his family and their 100-acre working farm on Pender Island. He has remained at the *News* as its publisher ever since.

THE RICHMOND NEWS

Because soft-spoken Bill Lam has a strong competitive nature, the *Richmond News* came into being; surviving against heavy odds and finally prospering.

Lam followed a curious route before finally arriving on the banks of the Fraser River.

Along the way, he attended college in New Orleans before moving on to the University of Missouri, where he received a bachelor of journalism and masters of communications degrees.

He seemed destined to get into the newspaper business.

"I always figured news was a very important part of my life," he recounts. "As a kid, I put newspaper clippings aside and was always intrigued by world events. My English wasn't too bad and I felt it might be a way of making a living."

After university, he worked in his home country Belize, then London and Brussels. During a visit to Vancouver, where one of his five sisters was living, he decided that British Columbia would be a great place to settle down.

After freelancing and working for the *North Shore News*, Lam decided he wanted to be a publisher.

"I saw newspapers as a sound business proposition, so I started looking around for an area where the business people believed in supporting newspapers."

He decided the growing community in Richmond could support another paper, and a defunct paper called the *Richmond News-Advertiser* was for sale, so Lam jumped and called the paper the *Richmond News*. It was 1977.

When he sold his first ad, one column by three inches, "I felt I had conquered the world."

The paper's breakthrough came in 1980. The basement office flooded and Lam checked the possibility of relocating to the retail heavy No. 3 Road.

"We had to be more visible."

The moved proved to be very wise. The sign out front worked like a giant advertising billboard and circulation grew. But the paper's staff also worked hard at improving editorial content.

In 1982, Ralph Hall, a veteran community newspaper editor/columnist, joined the paper and helped build the paper's reputation journalistically. Hall is still with the *News*.

Lam's biggest problem was getting major advertisers to commit. Eventually, even that turned around, coupled with membership into the BCYCNA. Lam knew then that the *News* was a major player.

After the *News* had moved to new a larger office on River Road, the competition, *The Review*, was sold to the Trinity chain, which was being challenged by the Now network of papers.

"It was then that I decided to sell majority ownership since it would have been virtually impossible for an independent publication to go up against that."

After long and tough negotiations with the Now network, a deal was closed in 1992 in which Lam retained a minority interest.

Lam stepped down as publisher soon after and is now with VanNet distribution. The *News* is still going strong.

THE RICHMOND REVIEW

Less than 50 years ago, Richmond was a sleepy farming and salmon fishing island community. Today it's more known for its booming Asian shopping district and it's hi-tech industry, flanked by an international airport enjoying a boom of its own.

Covering these dramatically changing islands is a serious challenge, but *The Richmond Review* has moved with the times, retaining its position as community newspaper of record since its inception in 1932.

The story goes that the community got its name from pioneer farmer Hugh McRoberts who named his farm in 1862 "Richmond." The name stuck.

When W.R. Carruthers, an unemployed printer, decided in 1932 to produce a newspaper for his community of 7,000, he likely didn't know the legacy he would leave behind.

The first issue of *The Richmond Review* was published on April 1, 1932. The four-page weekly hit the streets Fridays, featuring local news and advertising.

Carruthers' tenure, however, was short lived. The demands of producing a newspaper were too much for Carruthers so he sold it after printing only two copies to Ethel Caswell Tibbits, who had helped him put together the first two issues.

Although the paper was available by subscription for $1.50 per year, 1,200 extra copies were printed and distributed free each week, under the direction of O.D. Tibbits, *The Richmond Review's* first circulation manager.

Ethel Tibbits, a former journalist for the *Vancouver Province*, returned to Lulu Island, where she also helped keep a store with her husband. But after buying *The Review*, she devoted much of her time to running the newspaper, injecting it with a brave amount of personality. The paper grew both in prominence and in size, becoming a forum and a leader for the growing community it served.

Tibbits stayed with *The Review*, guiding it through the Depression and the Second World War until she retired in 1948.

The Review then went through a number of owners until 1963 when Herbert F. Gates, a former *Vancouver Sun* circulation manager bought *The Review* as a retirement hobby.

In those days, Richmond quickly established itself as a prime suburb of Vancouver. New shops and malls were built, its population soared and *The Review's* circulation grew with it. Gates first published the weekly paper with 2,400 copies. The circulation later increased to almost 10,000, before topping 15,000.

The broadsheet was the paper of choice, easily beating out large Vancouver dailies, and touting itself as "Canada's largest twice-weekly paid-circulation newspaper."

The Review switched to a tabloid newspaper in 1992 and moved publication dates from three days back to two. Today, *The Review* has a circulation of 44,100, serving a community of almost 155,000. But it hasn't forgotten its humble beginnings.

In recognition of Ethel Tibbits' pursuit of truth and justice, *The Review* annually honors Richmond's *Women of The Year*, in categories of sports, arts, community service and business. The name of the award that has come to mean the highest honor for women of Richmond: The Ethel Tibbits Award.

THE SECHELT REPORTER (SUNSHINE COAST REPORTER)

The *Sechelt Reporter* is the new kid on the block. The newspaper started up with its first issue on April 7, 1997. Since then it has grown to be one of the largest papers on the Sunshine Coast and in brilliant full colour, too.

With a circulation of about 14,000 from Port Mellon to Egmont, a dozen employees and a handful of columnists, the *Reporter*, which has an office about a block from the beach, hopes to continue being the "voice of the Sunshine Coast."

SQUAMISH CHIEF

Newspapers in Squamish have a long and storied history, featuring some of the best known characters in the industry. The *Squamish Standard* was published just prior to the First World War. Just before the Second World War, the legendary Margaret L. (Ma)

Murray and her husband started up the *Howe Sound News*. It was printed in Lillooet; home of her fabled *Bridge River Lillooet News*, but featured news from all the small communities in the Howe Sound area. It was discontinued in the war years.

Then in 1952, William Willoughby came from Terrace to start the *Squamish Advance*, which featured Rose Tatlow as editor. Forced after six years to give up the business by illness, Willoughby sold it to Cloudesley S. Q. Hoodspith of West Vancouver, who brought in Jack Wuttunes as editor. The paper, called the *Howe Sound Squamish Times*, continued to grow in the community, appearing a few times in tabloid format before switching to broadsheet. The four-page publication expanded to six or eight pages as more businesses started to realize the value of advertising.

Tatlow came back as editor in 1963, becoming assistant publisher a few years later and the growth continued. By 1967 the *Times* was ready for home delivery, jumping to a circulation of about 2,000, and over the years it won many of the most prestigious provincial and national awards in the newspaper industry. Tatlow gathered six national awards for her editorial pages, and the *Squamish Times* was twice named best all-round paper in its circulation category. Along the way, Tatlow became the first woman president of the B.C. and Yukon Community Newspapers Association.

On May 6, 1991, the first edition of the *Squamish Chief* hit the streets, with the cheeky slogan "Ahead of the *Times*." The *Chief* was published by Bob Doull of Whistler Printing and Publishing, a division of WestMount Press Ltd., with Cam Purdy as the first editor, Jeanneke Van Hattem as sales manager, and 10 staff people.

At that time, with papers in Whistler, Golden, Invermere, Banff, Canmore and Jasper, Doull says he was reluctant to start a paper in Squamish. But the ongoing requests from residents in the community could not be ignored.

A week later, a front page story in the *Chief* announced that Hoodspith had sold the *Squamish Times* and its sister papers, the *North Shore Citizen* and *Whistler This Week*, to British publishing giant Trinity International Holdings plc. Trinity already owned some 20 weekly papers in B.C. and Alberta, mostly in the Lower Mainland and Fraser Valley.

The *Chief* continued to grow, and went from free home delivery to paid circulation. Then, on February 8, 1993, the *Squamish Times* closed its doors.

Squamish has continued to grow as a community, being in an ideal location between jobs in Vancouver and the best winter skiing in North America just up the road in Whistler. The residential growth in Squamish has boosted the *Chief's* circulation to more than 4,300 copies per week.

In August 1996, Penny Graham left Revelstoke to become the *Chief's* publisher. In 1987, Rose Tatlow once again dug her old typewriter out of mothballs to write a historical column for the *Chief* and it quickly became one of the most popular features in the paper until her death in July, 1998.

WestMount Press Ltd., the parent company of the *Chief*, which includes 19 weekly papers in B.C. and Alberta, sold the group to Bowes Publishers, a division of Sun Media Corporation. They publish numerous weekly newspapers and two daily papers in Alberta, as well as other daily and weekly papers, shopping guides and magazines in British Columbia, Saskatchewan, Manitoba, Ontario and Florida.

Subsequent to the finalization of that deal, Whistler Printing and Publishing, which included the *Chief*, the *Whistler Question* and the *Bridge River-Lillooet News*, was sold by Bowes to Lower Mainland Publishing who in turn sold it to Madison Holdings Ltd.—a testament to the ever-changing face of community newspapers in British Columbia.

—Al Price

SURREY LEADER

Change is the one constant at the *Surrey Leader*. The enormous changes in the newspaper since 1971 are a reflection of the huge changes in the community it serves. Surrey's population was about 100,000 in 1971. It has now more than tripled, with more than 300,000 Surrey residents recorded in the 1996 census. Surrey has officially become a city. Vast suburban areas have become urbanized. SkyTrain has linked North Surrey to downtown Vancouver.

All these changes have been reflected in the pages of the *Leader*, and in its approach to covering its vast community.

Photo by Evan Seal, Surrey Leader.

In 1971, the *Leader* was a once-weekly, paid-circulation broadsheet newspaper that was delivered by mail to approximately 5,000 subscribers. The *Leader's* offices were in Cloverdale, one of Surrey's five official town centres.

Partners and co-publishers George Coupland and Stan McKinnon owned the newspaper. Coupland handled advertising and production, with McKinnon looking after the editorial side of the business.

Increased competition and the challenge of keeping up with a rapidly changing community were at times overwhelming, particularly after Coupland retired in the mid-1970s. Stan McKinnon and his wife Jeanette continued to manage the business, while Stan retained his duties as editor and still found time to cover Surrey council every Monday night.

He began looking for a way to keep the *Leader* viable and better able to keep up with all the changes in the community. He approached Hacker Press Ltd. of Abbotsford, which had printed the *Leader* since it went offset in the mid-1960s, and a deal was struck.

Hacker Press, a subsidiary of Liverpool Daily Post and Echo, bought the *Leader* and began publishing it in January 1979. Brian McCristall, editor of the *Abbotsford News*, was named publisher-editor, with McKinnon remaining as news editor.

The paper remained a paid-circulation weekly broadsheet, but soon a variety of approaches to increase circulation were tried, and carrier delivery was started. By 1982, the *Leader* had converted to a free-distribution weekly tabloid, with distribution expanded to include North Delta, an integral part of the marketplace.

The *Leader* became a twice-weekly broadsheet in late 1983, when it began publishing a Sunday edition. By 1984, with the demise of several competitors and a prolonged strike at Vancouver's two daily newspapers, the *Leader* was firmly established as Surrey's primary newspaper.

Stan McKinnon retired in 1984 after 48 years with the *Leader*, and continued as a columnist for several years until he was elected to Surrey council. Frank Bucholtz became news editor, and was named editor in 1986.

In 1983, Barbara Baniulis joined the newspaper in the front office. She was named sales supervisor in 1984, and publisher in 1987.

The *Leader* moved its office from Cloverdale to Whalley in September 1983. The move was a reflection of the *Leader's* growing strength in the North Surrey-North Delta marketplace, where most of the population resides.

The late 1980s were a period of steady growth and consolidation for the *Leader*. The parent company, now known as Trinity International, purchased the neighbouring *Peace Arch News* of White Rock and the *Langley Times* in 1985 and 1986, allowing for more integrated advertising sales in the fast-growing southern suburbs of Greater Vancouver.

The opening of the Alex Fraser Bridge and new highway links in 1986 and the coming of SkyTrain to Surrey in 1990 established more direct connections to Vancouver and added to Surrey and Delta growth.

Duane Geddes became publisher of the *Leader* in 1991. Andrew Holota took over as editor in 1993. The *Leader* has in recent years won numerous awards, including best newspaper in Canada and best newspaper in B.C..

Frank Teskey (publisher), Marlyn Graziano (editor) and Louise McKnight (sales manager), The Now.

In January 1997, ownership of the *Leader* and other members of the Metro Valley Newspaper Group returned to Canada, when Black Press Ltd. purchased Trinity International's Canadian holdings.

Candy Hodson was named publisher of the *Leader* in November 1997, after a stint as advertising manager. Arlie McClurg was named advertising manager and associate publisher a short time later.

The latest change at the *Leader* is the establishment of a third edition in April 1998. The *Leader* now publishes every Wednesday, Friday and Sunday. Its circulation is 83,000.

As the *Leader* looks back on 70 years of publication, it looks forward to many more changes in one of B.C.'s most dynamic and vibrant cities.

SURREY/ WHITE ROCK/ NORTH DELTA, NOW COMMUNITY

As the communities it serves have grown, so has the *Now Community* newspaper, in Surrey, White Rock and North Delta.

The first issue — a broadsheet — hit the streets on January 8, 1984. It was part of a new group of community newspapers, the *Now* chain, which was started by ex-employees of the *Columbian* after it folded. It was a Wednesday paper, initially delivered to 45,000 households. It later became a tabloid and continued as a weekly until the next decade. Pat Cooper was the editor of the first *Surrey-North Delta Now*, which was produced out of a central office in New Westminster. (That office was "home" to the other *Now* newspapers, which served New Westminster, Burnaby and Coquitlam, Port Coquitlam and Port Moody).

But as Surrey and North Delta grew, so did the newspaper and the need for its own office south of the Fraser River became apparent. And so the *Now* moved into Surrey in 1987. The composing room remained in the New Westminster office, but that move was the beginning of a strong local identity for the newspaper — an identity that has been forged through the years by dedicated employees who realized that being a community newspaper means first and foremost being a part of the community.

And in the case of the *Surrey-North Delta Now*, that meant being part of a growing community. It didn't take long before the circulation increased to 50,000 and by 1988 it was up to 63,000.

Surrey was quickly becoming known as British Columbia's fastest-growing city and soon there were even rumblings that it would eclipse Vancouver as the province's largest city. By 1991 the *Now* seized the opportunities offered by that growth and launched a weekend edition. In 1992, the circulation was again increased — this time to 80,000. As the paper grew, so did its staff and that required a move to new offices in August 1993. But the biggest change at the *Now* came in April 1994, when the communities of South Surrey and White Rock were brought into the fold and the paper began delivering to 105,000 households twice a week.

The move into South Surrey and White Rock was significant: for the first time ever, there was a newspaper that covered the City of Surrey entirely. The imaginary boundary that had been drawn between the north and south ends of the city had been erased; at the same time, however, the identity of separate communities within the city was recognized. Indeed, one of the great strengths of the *Now Community* (as the paper was re-named) is its ability to cover the entire area while helping the smaller communities within it retain their own identities.

This is accomplished with zoned advertising pages accompanied by editorial components that truly reflect the smaller communities in Surrey, White Rock and North Delta. The importance of customizing the newspaper for specific communities has proven so great, in fact, that the newspaper took further steps in 1995 with a major redesign. Further zoning, in which page one and page three are customized for two very different, yet linked markets, followed. For that reason, when the *Now* lands on a doorstep in North Surrey or North Delta, it is seen as the paper of record in those communities. The very same day, as it lands on doorsteps in South Surrey and White Rock, it is the paper of record there as well. It is their community newspaper, and it speaks to them.

That formula has not only won the *Now* accolades and support within the communities it serves, but from our profession as well — an achievement which reflects on every employee at the *Now*, where success has come from dedication and hard work, but mostly from doing what community newspapers do best: reflecting the lives of those we serve.

VANCOUVER COURIER

The Courier, like so many papers across B.C. and the Yukon, has a long and interesting history. In 1998, the paper commissioned Lisa Smedman to research and write a comprehensive history of the Courier. What follows is just part of what Smedman discovered and wrote about, but it reflects what a great many newspaper people have experienced over the years.

The year was 1908, and anything seemed possible. Point Grey had just seceded from Vancouver to form a separate municipality, and in the riverfront settlement of Eburne (today known as Marpole), new businesses were being built in anticipation of a fresh-water harbour. Richmond had yet to be subdivided, and Lulu Island (today home of the Vancouver International Airport) was a farming community.

The newspaper that would one day be known as the *Courier* was launched in the spring of 1908 as a four-page paper; a single broadsheet folded in two. Alfred H. Lewis, a journeyman printer, founded it. Annie Lewis (who shared a residential address with Alfred) is listed in the 1908 Vancouver directory as a bookbinder, and may also have been involved in the venture.

Ninety years ago, Point Grey was a settlement of approximately 100 families. The Native village Snauq occupied reserve lands that today are home to the Vancouver Museum and Planetarium. The area was still considered remote; the electric tramline along 4th Avenue would not open until the following year. The Jericho Golf Club had laid out a nine-hole course on land formerly owned by lumberman Jerry Rogers (at "Jerry's Cove" which had become shortened to "Jericho"), the Industrial School on 4th Avenue housed "bad boys," and cows grazed on what would one day become the University Endowment Lands.

The 12,000-acre municipality boasted two schools with a total of 43 students.

The offices and printing presses of the *Gazette* were in Eburne, a settlement that straddled the north and south banks of the Fraser River between the Sea Island and Lulu Island bridges. The town was built around the Manitoba Lumber Company sawmill. Its business core also included the Dominion Grocery, Gordon's hardware store, Clugston's blacksmith shop, the Griggs Brothers general store and Swift's Abattoir. The Delta Club was across the railway tracks, and the post office was located on Sea Island, in a general store run by Sidney Bell (who later built the first store in Kerrisdale). There were also approximately a dozen houses.

In October of 1908, the weekly newspaper was sold to Herbert Beeman and J.E.L. St. Clere. But a conflict of interest soon arose. St. Clere was a councillor with the municipality of Point Grey, and would be disqualified from this position if the newspaper accepted municipal advertising, and Beeman was the municipal clerk. And so the paper was sold to Richard S. Ford of the *Saturday Sunset*, a Vancouver weekly newspaper that had been founded in 1907, and that later served as the springboard for the launching of the *Vancouver Sun* in 1912. Ford would continue in the newspaper business until 1915, when the *Saturday Sunset* folded. He then went into the business of importing goods from the Orient.

In November of 1908, one month after Ford purchased the *Gazette*, the newspaper changed hands once again. The new owner was James Alexander Paton, who had come west to try his hand at ranch-

Vancouver Courier, *September 13, 1998. Photo by Randall Cosco.*

ing, placer mining, construction, shopkeeping, and eventually, publishing. He renamed the paper the *Point Grey Gazette*.

"I became the proprietor of a flourishing weekly newspaper with
108 subscribers, mostly deadheads or complimentaries," Paton later
recalled in an article published in the early 1930s. "(The newspaper
also had) several columns of phantom advertising – phantom because
they appeared in the newspaper but not in the cash box.

"At the close of the first year .. the *Point Grey Gazette* had about 140
paid-up subscribers which included everybody that lived in Point
Grey, about half the families in Richmond municipality, and the balance Point Grey property owners."

Alfred H. Lewis, the newspaper's original owner, continued in the printing business, as owner of the Lewis Printing & Publishing Company, located at 4107 Westminster Ave. The business was later known as A.H. Lewis & Sons, the sons being Albert and William. The 1914 Vancouver directory lists this company as publisher of a newspaper called the *Gazette*, so Lewis may have still had some interest in the paper. In the 1922 directory, Alfred H. Lewis lists his occupation as journalist.

Beeman, the paper's second owner, continued as a columnist for the newspaper until 1910, writing under the name "The Friar." He also wrote poetry.

In 1908, Paton attended a meeting of the Eburne Ratepayers Association, at which the industrialization of the north arm of the Fraser River and the development of planned residential communities in "virgin" and "unspoiled" Point Grey were discussed.

He later wrote: "These two projects were enough to inspire me with the possibility of a mission of service sufficient for the establishment of the *Point Grey Gazette*, and from its first issue, those two points were the unswerving goal of the little newspaper. . . In season and out, dredging the North Arm and a planned Point Grey was dinned into the minds of the subscribers who read the paper. And they did read it for it contained an item of their every action, whether trials, tribulations or rejoicings. It was a gazette of the daily life of a pioneer people."

The first year of the *Gazette* was an exciting one. The municipality of Point Grey was growing as more settlers arrived. Paton wrote: "By 1909 the future of the municipality was assured. The Shaughnessy development was under way, and the population was increasing at a great rate. By the subterfuge of borrowing a couple of children, the needed seven had been secured and the Kerrisdale school built."

The fledgling municipality fought with both the B.C. Electric Railway (which provided electric tram service to Greater Vancouver) and the B.C. Telephone Company. "One of the bitterest struggles was that which resulted in a pay phone being installed on the front verandah of Syd Bell's store at Kerrisdale so the populace could have access at any hour to call the doctor," Paton recalled.

The newspaper also covered the question of whether streetcar service to Point Grey should be a B.C.E.R. franchise for the whole of

Greater Vancouver (an option the paper supported) or whether it should come under the ownership of the Point Grey municipality.

Negotiations with the B.C.E.R. deadlocked when the company refused to grant concessions demanded by the Greater Vancouver Transportation Committee, which was seeking a five-cent fare throughout Greater Vancouver, a percentage of gross earnings (rather than net earnings), a reduction in interurban fares, and the laying of new tracks. Angry Point Grey councillors said the municipality should be negotiating on its own with the B.C.E.R. The debate was so heated that the question would become an election platform in 1912.

In those early days, the *Gazette* was a solid booster of "progress" and supported "building for the future." The newspaper's editorials pushed for increased spending on roads and parks, for dredging of the Fraser River, for the establishment of municipal water and sewer service in Point Grey and Richmond, and for the appropriation of land on which to build the University of B.C. Despite the fact that Paton was an avid golfer, the paper opposed an attempt by the Shaughnessy Golf Club to get a standard assessment "at the expense of the ratepayers."

The *Gazette's* editorial stand was often at odds with the opinions of the Point Grey municipal councillors. In retaliation, the municipality refused to advertise with the newspaper.

Paton recalled: "I ran foul of the Point Grey Council about the same time (as the B.C.E.R. scrap) and was deprived of municipal advertising for about a year, and, as a consequence, had to tighten up my belt a couple of notches."

In a 1923 editorial, Paton wrote: "As far back as the first year of the *Gazette's* career the council disciplined the paper by withholding advertising. In the year 1912 we didn't get a dollar's worth of business because we fought the election of the successful. Strangely enough, that election was fought on the B.C.E.R. franchise and the people elected a council who told them that, if elected, they could make a better agreement. They didn't fulfill their election promise, however, for the agreement is practically the same one …

"As recently as last year there was a period during which advertising was withheld from the *Gazette* by the municipality…

". . . the time was when advertisers were able to intimidate publishers by threatening to withdraw their patronage. This did not last very long, however, as wise advertisers saw that the only publication of value was the one respected by subscribers. Publishers found that no one liked a weak publication, and the very subserviency to the advertiser lost the advertiser patronage by ruining the character of the paper.

". . . my biggest advertiser didn't bother to threaten, it just withheld business."

In 1911, the *Point Grey Gazette* was published on a paid subscription basis from offices in the Clugston-Barton block on Eburne Ave. A single issue cost five cents, and a year's subscription was one dollar. The eight-page weekly broadsheet covered Point Grey, Eburne, Lulu Island and Sea Island, and offered subscriptions to readers elsewhere in Canada and in the United Kingdom, Newfoundland, New Zealand and "certain other British possessions" for an additional 50 cents per year.

"It was rather a lot of fun trying to keep up a front and eat at the same time," Paton later recalled. "No one knows the number of times the issuing of the *Gazette* rested on the receipt of an unsolicited want ad backed up by a quarter."

In 1911, the development of the Fraser River by the Vancouver Harbour and Dock Company was very much in the news, as was the imminent opening of a branch of the Royal Bank in Eburne. Another top news story was the increasing population of B.C. The census figures for 1911 showed a population increase of more than 100 per cent, to 362,768 persons.

Newspaper columns included "Girls and Boys," a roundup of jokes and games by "Cousin Doris," "The Kitchenette," a collection of recipes and cooking tips, and "Between You and Me," which looked at fashion and health.

In a 1930 article, Paton commended the early residents of Point Grey for their community spirit. "The *Gazette* helped to create this spirit by keeping the people fully informed on all questions of municipal interest. The Point Grey citizens were sold on the advantages of town planning long before the legislation was passed that allowed it to be put into effect."

The newspaper's first paid reporter was J.T. Bartlett, who later worked for the *Province*. Another early reporter was Tommy Putman, who was also a columnist.

Paton wrote: "When I first started the paper the question of getting circulation resolved itself into a problem of bringing prospective subscribers into the prescribed area—bringing the mountain to Mohamet as it were. The advertisers were always demanding increased circulation, and merely stating that the paper had the 'largest circulation of any paper published in Point Grey' was not altogether sufficient."

In the early part of the decade, the *Gazette* devoted much of its coverage to local politics. National politics also occasionally made the news, particularly when the Liberals or Tories held a local convention. When it came to world events, the focus was on the British Empire; the newspaper devoted a front page in 1911 to the coronation of King George V.

Local news stories focused on the opening of new businesses and a local post office, on the development of roads, sewer and water systems, on new tramlines and expansions to the telephone service. Meetings of the Boy's Brigade and church teas were covered, and lists of the guests at local hotels were published. The social columns published news of who was away on vacation, who was entertaining visitors, and local residents who had recently returned from trips abroad. There were also stories of automobile and tram crashes, holdups, murders, fires, and deaths or injuries caused by dynamite used to clear stumps.

With the outbreak of World War I, the focus of the *Gazette's* news coverage shifted to the war in Europe. The *Gazette* published letters sent home by soldiers at the front, published an eyewitness account of the Halifax explosion of 1917, and told stories of servicemen who had received medals or who had made the "supreme sacrifice." Local Red Cross efforts were supported, and the citizens of Point Grey were exhorted to reduce their consumption of wheat and bacon—foods that were shipped overseas to feed the men in the trenches. The social pages now also mentioned local soldiers who had returned home on leave.

In 1915, Paton enlisted in the Seaforth Highlanders and sold the *Gazette* to Ernest L. Woodruff, who became its publisher. The paper expanded into the Delta area, and changed its name to the *Weekly Gazette*.

Paton would later boast of the *Gazette's* wartime record in a 1920 editorial: "All those connected with the *Weekly Gazette* are justly proud of the war record of that publication, for out of the small staff, no less than six put on khaki and went to the front, and that long before the Conscription Act was brought into operation. Out of that number, one paid the supreme sacrifice (a press feeder with the surname Kent who served as a private during the war), and thus became one of that noble band who gave up all that was most dear on earth in the gallant fight for Freedom, Honor and Justice; while two were wounded (Paton and printer W. Flemming).

"We think this truly constitutes a record anywhere in the world, when the percentage of men employed is taken into consideration. Why, it practically meant that the whole staff went to the front, and those who were left behind were physically unfit to pass the doctor."

Those who went off to war included reporter Thomas Putman, who, after being rejected three times for the front line due to defective eyesight, joined the Railway Troops. When due to be shipped out to England in 1917, Putman again managed to stay close to the front lines by obtaining a position as a stenographer in the Orderly Room of the Canadian General Base at Etaples. Archie Cook, who worked in the newspaper's circulation department, joined the artillery, while Fred Clugston, also from the circulation department, managed to join up despite being three months under 18 years of age.

By 1917, the newspaper's name had been expanded to *Weekly Gazette and Home News*. In September of 1917, its publishers were listed as W. Hamar Greenwood and J.B. Sunderland, and the paper was located at 929 Birks Building, in Vancouver. Dorothy G. Bell became the newspaper's editor in October of 1917.

During the war, Paton suffered a wound that cost him his leg. Upon his return from active service in 1918, he and co-owner P.F. Cooper purchased the newspaper back from Woodruff. Cooper, who lived in Point Grey, was described as: "a well known newspaper man, for the past 11 years engaged in journalistic work in Vancouver, having previously been connected with a number of eastern newspapers." Cooper continued to be listed as co-publisher of the *Weekly*

Gazette until February of 1920; after that, only Paton's name appears, under the title managing editor.

Woodruff went on to work for the J. Coughlan & Sons shipyard (he is listed as an employee there in the 1918 B.C. Directory). Woodruff later lists his occupation as printer, and as manager of the Educational Book Supply Company.

After purchasing the newspaper in December of 1918, Paton moved the offices of the *Weekly Gazette* to the Dominion Building, located on the corner of Hastings Street and Cambie, which at the time was the tallest building in the British Empire. Just across Hastings Sreet was the *Province* Building, built by the publisher of the *News-Advertiser*, one of Vancouver's early daily newspapers that began publication in 1886. Competition between the dailies was fierce during this period, with the *News-Advertiser* going head to head against the *Province* (founded in 1898), the *Vancouver Sun* (founded in 1912) and the *World* (founded in 1888), which occupied the World Tower building at Beatty and Pender streets. (The building was later known as the Sun Tower, after the *Vancouver Sun* occupied it from 1937 to 1965).

Ray E. Hutcherson, a fellow soldier of the 72nd Battallion (to which Paton belonged) joined the paper in 1919. An editorial described the reorganization that was taking place:

"The *Weekly Gazette* is to undergo a general reorganization and more news is promised, particularly to the subscribers of Richmond and Delta municipalities ...An arrangement was completed during the past week by which Mr. R.E. Hutcherson, lately returned from overseas, assumed charge of our interests there and a lively subscription and advertising campaign may be looked forward to.

"Being a local boy as far as Delta is concerned, he will be in an exceptionally fine position to reflect the views of the residents of that locality upon current events."

During the last two years of the decade, the paper regularly ran editorials urging the provincial government to do more for the returned soldier. The column "Farm, Furrow and Field" provided notes for the soldier turned farmer. Fashion returned to the newspaper with the column "The Women's Page." Also in the news was the Spanish Influenza epidemic of 1918, which claimed a number of lives and necessitated the establishment of temporary flu hospitals.

As the decade drew to a close, the former soldiers settled back into their lives as editors, reporters and printers. The *Weekly Gazette* had not only survived but thrived during its first decade in business, expanding first into Richmond and then into Delta.

In January 1920, Paton wrote: "A weekly newspaper is a recognized institution, as can be shown from the fact that here in Canada alone there were at the close of 1919 a total of 1,073 weekly newspapers in existence, of which number 53 are published in British Columbia. The number of daily papers in B.C. totals 14 . . ."

In July 1920, Paton noted that, while most weeklies were increasing the cost of a year's subscription to $2, the *Weekly Gazette* was continuing to offer subscriptions for $1.50 per year. "A larger paper is contemplated in the near future. . . . Subscribe now and help the *Gazette* carry on the good work."

But times were tight. The disruption caused by the Great War, when no less than six of the newspaper's small staff enlisted, was still making its impact felt. In February 1921, Paton wrote: "The war period interfered with the advancement of the *Gazette*. The attempt to re-establish the paper has not met with any distinguishable degree of enthusiasm. In fact, at times hostility seems to prevail in certain quarters for reasons not yet made plain.

"An attempt has been made to run the *Gazette* as an independent organ. This attitude will be continued though it appears to be a costly one . . .

"Two years of endeavor have been spent in the attempt to increase the size of the paper to pre-war size in order that we may be enabled to give the service the district deserves."

Among those who returned to the newspaper after war service was the writer "Touchstone," who offered "interesting and chatty comments on local and other topics" in his column "The Passing Show." A July 1920 newspaper announced: "'Touchstone' has the whole world for his gleaning and we are sure that his observations, whether caustic or otherwise, will be as much appreciated now as they were before the Great War .. and will become a permanent feature of the paper in the future."

The *Gazette* continued to support progress and development. Paton was firmly behind the creation of the University of B.C., and in 1920 distributed the newspaper free of charge for one month to boost public support for this project. The effort was successful, and in February 1921, he wrote: "Such public interest was awakened that the question was strongly placed before the Government with the result that a definite scheme has been decided upon by the Government . . ."

The following summer, the "Great Trek" of 1922 would see students (many of them returned servicemen) occupy the UBC campus and demand that construction of its buildings be completed.

In May 1921, the *Gazette* was forced to cease publication for two months due to a printers' strike that was "raging throughout the North American continent." When the newspaper resumed publication on July 9, an editorial announced: "Happily, owing to other arrangements, we are enabled to produce this issue of the *Gazette* and we are in high hopes of being able to continue the publication of the paper in the future.

"That the strike is altogether unjustified—more especially at this present time of unemployment, stringency and depression—the following facts as to its cause, we think will convince all unprejudiced persons.

"The minimum scale of pay throughout the city stood at $40.50 per week of 48 hours. The demand of the men is for a reduction of hours by four, bringing the time down from 48 hours to 44 hours per week, with the same rate of pay $40.50.

"There are thousands of men in Canada today who would think themselves remarkably well off to be getting $40.50 a week, even for longer hours and much harder work."

In 1923, the *Gazette* returned to its Point Grey roots, relocating its business office in Kerrisdale at 5675 West Boulevard. (It would later move down the block to 5703 West Boulevard.) By 1925 the newspaper reflected this move by abandoning the name *Weekly Gazette*, in favour of its previous name: the *Point Grey Gazette*.

In 1925, the newspaper experimented with an innovative circulation policy. After years of distributing the paper only to paying subscribers, in June of that year 1,500 copies of the *Gazette* was distributed free of charge to homes in Strathcona, Kerrisdale and Magee.

The newspaper announced: "We are doing this in response to requests from our advertisers that we give them a circulation sufficient for their needs in the immediate vicinity of their stores. In printing fifteen hundred extra copies . . . we are making it possible for them to convey a weekly message to every resident, every possible customer, in these large districts.

"This is not a transient flare in our advertising flame. We mean to keep it up. We guarantee to continue this free circulation throughout the summer, at least. If our fellow tradesmen will cooperate we will continue it indefinitely."

The practice of using free distribution to increase a newspaper's circulation (which in turn makes it more attractive to the advertisers whose ad purchases pay the costs of publishing it) was not generally adopted by community newspapers until the 1980s. This innovative experiment also allowed the *Gazette* to increase its news content.

At the same time, the newspaper devoted the whole of its back page to advertising. Paton wrote: "This page is now, in reality, an advertising sheet, something for which local business men have been asking for some time.

"Each week the personnel of advertisers represented on this page changes. We wish to give every merchant an opportunity of using this page. If the sheet is filled before we are able to get in touch with you, however, do not think that you have lost your opportunity of identifying yourself with this excellent advertising vehicle. We will be glad to make a space for you on one of our inside pages. The circulation is the same for an inside page as an outer one, and there is the added advantage, in the former case, of securing a space adjacent to news matter."

To increase its paid circulation, the newspaper offered special gifts to subscribers. In 1923, subscribers were promised a six-inch Tokinabe porcelain vase in an Egyptian pattern similar to that found on the grave goods of the recently excavated King Tutankhamen. Earlier, the newspaper had offered a "dandy, brand new two-bladed, stag-handled pocket knife" to boys who could round up three new subscribers or subscription renewals.

During the summer of 1925, UBC student Earle Birney (who would later become one of Canada's most prominent poets) was hired as associate editor of the newspaper. When Birney returned to school in September, Clifford H. Dowling became the *Gazette's* associate editor.

News stories from that year included the development of the

A bear was shot today as it grazed in a meadow near town. Authorities said the bear was a potential threat to a nearby residential area and had to be killed. And in other news, a convicted sex offender, on early parole, was arrested again. The suspect, who authorities say is not a threat to society, remains free on bail.

Rodgers ©96

Capilano water main and intake. The Janet Smith murder of the previous year and the more recent kidnapping of Chinese houseboy Wong Foon Sing, who found the body, continued to be top news items. Publisher J.A. Paton would later face criminal charges as a co-conspirator to the kidnapping – but while the dailies ran this story, the *Gazette* never once mentioned that criminal charges had been laid against its publisher.

In August 1926, the *Gazette* merged with a rival community newspaper, the *Fairview Citizen*. The *Gazette* moved into the offices formerly occupied by the Citizen, at 1451 West Broadway.

W. Cowper Harris, who served for many years as its editor, had founded the *Citizen* around the same time as the *Point Grey Gazette*. Harris also had an avid interest in floriculture. Even prior to the amalgamation of the two newspapers, he had been a contributing writer to the *Gazette* with his column "In the Garden."

The merged publication (which would for a time be known as the *Citizen Gazette*) was sold to James K. Falconer in December 1926. It was an eight-page broadsheet with a circulation of 7,500 and served Point Grey, Fairview, University Hill and parts of Richmond.

The new publisher wrote: "The *Point Grey Gazette* and the *Citizen* have been publishing in their respective districts for the past 18 years. During that period Fairview and Point Grey, lying in proximity to each other, have more or less grown together. Consequently it was felt that the two weekly newspapers amalgamated into one and circulated through both districts would have a greater public appeal than the two older papers published under their separate heads." Falconer promised a "weightier paper and consequently one which will stand better chances of being carefully read than the smaller sheets."

Paton continued to write on an occasional basis for the newspaper, contributing articles on the history of Point Grey, or commenting on issues of the day in his capacity as reeve of Point Grey.

A rival newspaper challenged the *Gazette* during the late '20s. The *Point Grey News* was established in January 1926, and operated from offices at 5745 West Boulevard. Owned by the Point Grey News Publishing Company, this rival paper was published on Fridays and, like the *Gazette*, cost 5 cents a copy or $2 per year. R. Richardson, who served as its business and advertising manager, headed it up.

The *Point Grey News* was still being published in 1928; a newspaper from October of that year still survives. Its distribution overlapped that of the *Gazette*; it was circulated in Shaughnessy, Kerrisdale, Dunbar Heights, West Grey, Almadene, University Hill, Richmond, and Marpole.

During the 1920s, regular columns in the *Point Grey Gazette* included "Hints for the Home," a collection of jokes called the "Whimsical Review," a collection of poetry under the heading "Literary Corner," world news briefs, and "The Pedlar's Pack."

In October 1926 the newspaper added a column by "well known dietitian" Dr. Frank McCoy that answered medical questions. The *Gazette* boasted that this was the first time this syndicated column had appeared in a Vancouver newspaper.

Editor Clifford Dowling wrote a regular column called "The Weekly Grind" which gradually increased in length; by 1927 it filled the entire front page of the paper. Dowling gave his personal slant on the international news stories of the day, including everything from the sensational Sacco-Vanzetti case (working class anarchists who were executed for a murder they said they did not commit) to "companionate marriages" – trial marriages of a one-year duration.

He wryly noted: "Lindsay and Wells might have done better to propound their marriage theories as predictions rather than suggestions. The rapid increase in the number of divorces is making towards just such a state as those two well known men have recommended."

When citizens expressed outrage over a billboard that showed a man and a woman "in a clinch," Dowling countered by calling it an "ideal of love." He wrote: "That picture is a work of art. It is one of the finest things that has ever been displayed on a local billboard."

Dowling was pro-lottery, and was critical of a movement to ban lotteries – "even those conducted for welfare work." His columns labelled the United States "one of the most crime-ridden nations in the semi-civilized world today."

The newspaper's social pages continued to thrive; the regular column "Items of Social and Personal Interest" noted local marriages, women's club picnics, and visits by out-of-town guests. The Scouts were well represented in the newspaper, with their own column, "Sea Scout Notes."

Other columns included "Above the Battle" by J. Buchanan Tonkin, which bemoaned the "lack of great men" in modern times, a column on home economics titled "Trouble-Saving Ideas," and "The Fashionscope" by Miss Wiles debated the merits of short versus long skirts.

In the entertainment section, it was announced that Barnum and Bailey would be bringing their combined show to Vancouver in August. The five-ring circus featured Pawah, the "sacred white pachyderm from Burma," as well as 90 zebras, camels and horses, and 43 elephants—more than 1,000 animals in all.

Despite the fact that it had been financially struggling a few years previously, in the latter half of the 1920s the *Gazette* prospered. The publisher noted that 1927 was "a big year for the *Point Grey Gazette*." Circulation had increased by 25 per cent over the previous 12-month period, to more than 10,000 per week. The paper was not only being read, but was making an impact. *Gazette* editorials were "quoted more frequently by the big city dailies than any other publication."

When the Depression hit Vancouver in the 1930s, the unemployed marched in the streets, protested at city hall, and occupied the post office, Hotel Georgia and Carnegie Library. With the highest per capita income in the city, and because it was at the end of the railway line, Vancouver proved a lure for the unemployed, who poured into the city at a rate of 40 to 50 a day. In Point Grey in 1930, the city's first relief crews were put to work clearing land.

Through it all, the weekly community paper that had been founded in 1908 continued to report the news. In this turbulent decade it was known by a variety of names—a legacy of the amalgamation of two different newspapers just a few years earlier. As the decade opened, the masthead of the newspaper read *Point Grey Gazette & the Citizen*. By 1935 the name had changed to *Point Grey News Gazette*. One year later the name had changed yet again, to *Fairview News Gazette*. But by 1939 the publication was back to its original name: *Point Grey Gazette*.

In 1930 the *Gazette* was an eight-page weekly tabloid newspaper. A single issue cost five cents, while a year's subscription was $2.

Publisher James K. ("Jim") Falconer continued to edit the newspaper, which was listed by the B.C. Directory as being owned by the Point Grey News Gazette Ltd., located at 2182 West 41st Ave.

Herbert W. ("Will") Reeder was president of this company by 1931, and by 1934 is listed as its managing editor. He also published the *Highland Echo*, another Vancouver weekly.

The Reeders had come to Vancouver in the late 1920s from the Prairies, where Will Reeder had homesteaded and served as a North-West Mounted Police officer. After moving to Vancouver, the whole family was involved in the production of the *Gazette*. Will's wife Ellen ("Nell") was in charge of the office, and proofread the galleys as they were printed. She also wrote the social and church news.

Their daughter Margaret (now Margaret Laycock) was officially listed as the company's stenographer in the B.C. Directory. Trained as a bindery worker, she operated the press and folding machine.

Their eldest son Herbert was its secretary-treasurer and advertising manager. He was also the newspaper's circulation manager.

In addition to editing the *Gazette*, Will Reeder was also the managing editor of *Western Canada Radio News*, a guide to radio programming that was published from the same office as the *Point Grey News Gazette*.

Over the period that the Reeders owned the *Gazette*, the office at 2182 West 41st Avenue was expanded three times to accommodate a linotype, press and large power cutter. Son Hedley Reeder recalls

Vancouver from the roof of the Hotel Vancouver, Georgia Street, circa 1901. City of Vancouver Archives, Dist. P 150, N. 127.

that his father "worked his butt off" to make the business profitable.

But in 1938 or 1939, the Reeders were forced to sell the *Gazette*. While he was unwilling to give details, Hedley said his father's decision to leave the *Gazette* was prompted by "politics," alluding to the fact that Will Reeder was a Liberal supporter. Hedley added that his father had to "walk away from the newspaper" when financial difficulties threatened to put it out of business.

Will Reeder continued in the newspaper business for a time; the 1941 B.C. Directory lists him as working for the *Vancouver Sun*. He later moved his family to Richmond, where he served as a charter president for two Kiwanis clubs and played the organ in local churches.

Albert E. Gibbs, a printer who had been in charge of the compositing room, became the next president of the *Point Grey Gazette*. He would continue working at the *Gazette* until 1941. He worked for a time under owner Morris Belkin, a young entrepreneur who used the *Gazette's* presses to custom-print cardboard boxes. According to his son, Gibbs quit in protest and started his own newspaper when it became clear that the *Gazette* would take second place to making a buck in the paper box business.

The newspaper that would one day be known as the *Courier* entered the 1940s as the *Point Grey News Gazette*. In 1940, James K. Falconer served as its advertising manager, and Albert E. Gibbs as its manager and director. The six-page broadsheet had a circulation of 5,700 and incorporated the *Western Canada Radio News Magazine* within its pages.

In 1938 or 1939, Morris J. Belkin purchased the Point Grey News Gazette Ltd., the company that owned the *Gazette*. He was a young entrepreneur, fresh out of university, who got his start in journalism by editing the UBC student newspaper the *Ubyssey* in the late 1930s.

Belkin used the newspaper's printing presses to found Belkin Paper Box Ltd., which custom printed boxes for the fashion and food industries. (As late as 1948, the address of Belkin Paper Box Ltd. is the same as that of the *Gazette*.)

Belkin also owned College Printers, a printing business which he reputedly purchased for $150 after his graduation from UBC. His partner in this venture was David G. Nelson. He would eventually use the presses at College Printers to print both the *Gazette* and the *Ubyssey*.

The *Gazette* (and later the *Courier*) would continue to be printed at College Printers until the 1980s; whenever Belkin sold the newspaper he included a clause in the purchase agreement that required it to be printed at College Printers.

By 1949 Belkin Paper Box Ltd. had moved to 1030 Kingsway, and the *Point Grey News Gazette* to 2305 West 41st Avenue. (It would remain at this address until 1973). Belkin went on to build his box printing business into a multi-million-dollar business. When the parent company, Belkin Inc., was sold to Paperboard Industries Corp in 1987 for $210 million it employed 2,600 people across Canada.

Another young university graduate purchased the *Point Grey News Gazette* in 1948. Harold R. Pinchin, who had graduated from UBC that year with a degree in commerce, had got his feet wet in the newspaper business by working part time for the *Highland Echo* while he was a student, selling advertising and printing, and occasionally writing the for *Echo*.

"As a matter of fact, the publisher of the *Echo*, Alex Holmes, loaned me the $1,000 to buy the *Gazette*," recalled Pinchin.

Pinchin had gotten to know Belkin because the *Ubyssey*, which Pinchin had edited, was printed in Belkin's printing shop. He heard from Belkin that the newspaper might be for sale.

"When I graduated, I decided that I had to tell the world how to save itself."

The *Gazette* had a small staff; Pinchin did the bulk of the writing and advertising sales. His former wife Shirley, who graduated from UBC's home economics program, worked in the front office and also wrote a cooking column. "(The *Gazette*) was primarily news, gossip, and any little political jargonings that were going on."

It was Pinchin who changed the name of the newspaper.

"The *Point Grey News Gazette* had a very long and distinguished history. I felt that it had some value. But we didn't circulate in Point Grey. We needed something that identified the paper more locally with the community, which was the rationale behind changing the name to *Kerrisdale Courier*."

Why did he choose that name?

"Courier. Runner. I had all of these little kids running around delivering the paper. So that was the *Kerrisdale Courier*."

Pinchin later had a partner. Philip A. Thiemer, originally an advertising salesman, was brought on board to manage the *Gazette* while Pinchin turned his attention to another newspaper he had recently purchased—the *Semiahmoo Sun*, which served White Rock. (He later renamed it the *White Rock Sun*.)

The pair was also producing the *News Gazette*, which served Vancouver's West End. This newspaper was published fortnightly (every two weeks) and was a four-page tabloid with a circulation of 5,000. Pinchin was the paper's managing editor, and Thiemer was its advertising manager.

The partnership between Pinchin and Thiemer came to an end shortly after Pinchin purchased the White Rock newspaper, around 1950.

"When I bought the White Rock paper, I in effect bought my own printing plant with the paper. I was looking to get to the point where I could control my own production."

In 1953, Thiemer sold the *Sun* and returned to school, moving to the United States to study graphics arts management at Carnegie Tech. He never returned to the newspaper business.

As the decade drew to a close and the war years receded, prosperity and growth were the buzzwords. A new era – and a new name – lay ahead for the *Courier* in the decade to come.

The newspaper formerly known as the *Point Grey Gazette* entered the 1950s with not only a new name but also a new publisher. In 1950 or 1951, the *Kerrisdale Courier* changed hands yet again when it was purchased by Kenneth Walker Edwards and his wife Elizabeth (Beth) Edwards.

The Edwards ran it as a husband and wife team until May of 1955, when Ken died after a lengthy illness at the age of 46.

Beth Edwards continued to publish the newspaper after her husband's death, serving as its editor until 1968.

Under the direction of editor and publisher Beth Edwards, the *Kerrisdale Courier* entered the 1960s as a folksy community newspaper, focused primarily on the Kerrisdale area, although it was also distributed in Shaughnessy, Shannon, Southlands, McKenzie Heights and Dunbar. The *Courier* continued to be published from the heart of Kerrisdale, in an office at 2265 West 41st Ave., throughout the 1960s.

In 1968, Edwards decided to sell the *Kerrisdale Courier*.

The newspaper was sold to William (Bill) Forst who took over the *Kerrisdale Courier* as of May 31, 1968. Described as a "well known newspaper man" who was "prominent in the newspaper business in Vancouver for many years," Forst was formerly managing editor of the daily *Province*. He had also worked at the *Province* as city editor, sports editor and news editor.

Forst had previously been involved in a venture to launch a new daily newspaper in Vancouver during a strike that hit the city's two dailies in the mid-1960s. His firm, William Forst & Associates, organized the editorial department for the *Vancouver Times*, which first appeared in the fall of 1964 and which survived for 11 months, until August of 1965. Forst was editorial director of the *Times*.

Preparing double track right-of-way for streetcar line on Fourth Avenue, 1909. City of Vancouver Archives, Kit. P. 23, N. 23.

One of the first things Forst did was to redesign the front page and change the name of the newspaper to the *Courier in Kerrisdale*. He then brought in a number of new writers, many of whom had worked for the dailies.

Tony Simnett, originally from England, had 15 years' experience as a reporter before joining the *Kerrisdale Courier* in 1969. He worked for the *Calgary Herald* and *Vancouver Sun*. An avid tennis and table tennis player, he played in the Davis Cup and ranked fifth in the United Kingdom.

Unlike Edwards, who preferred to focus on "happy events," Forst filled the newspaper with hard news—crime, fires, crashes and politics. In an editorial introducing himself to readers, he outlined the direction the *Courier* would take.

"The *Courier* appears today in a new format featuring some different material—but with the same principal objective – to serve the community in which it has for so long made its home. The activities, the projects, the business life and the problems of our neighbours will be our concern—as they should be the concern of every community newspaper worthy of the name."

Forst upped the circulation of the newspaper to 10,000 and announced: "A circulation campaign to build this lusty family of more than 30,000 potential readers has already been launched. The entire neighbourhood will soon be made aware of 'the new *Courier*.'"

In 1971, Granville Press Ltd published the *Courier*. In June 1973, the newspaper moved to 2025 West 42nd Ave.

In 1975, Robin Lecky purchased the newspaper (which by then had shortened its name to the *Courier*) from Jack Ferry. At the time, Ferry was a partner with Morris Belkin in College Printers. The newspaper moved yet again, to 5559 West Blvd.

Lecky, who had a background in copy writing, advertising and music production, was the son of a newspaperman. His father was an advertising and marketing director for the *Vancouver Sun*.

Other investors taking part in this purchase of the *Courier* included chartered accountant Mike Francis, who was once active in civic politics; Peter Hyndman (who was later forced to relinquish his *Courier* holdings when he won a provincial seat with the Social Credit party); Bill Lang, who worked for a brokerage firm before joining the newspaper; and Howard Eaton (who later sold his holdings when he became president of the Canadian Commercial and Industrial Bank in Edmonton).

In the spring of 1975, Lecky also purchased the original *West Ender*—a newspaper that had been started in July of 1951 by A.J. Arnold. Meanwhile, at the *Courier*, Peter Ballard and Phillip Hager joined the paper as advertising representatives in the spring of 1975.

Lecky continued to publish the *West Ender* and *Courier* as two separate newspapers, under their original names, until August 1975. He then combined the two under one umbrella, and gave each a new name. The *West Ender* became the *West End Courier*, while the original *Courier* was renamed the *West Side Courier*.

Cost of a single issue of the *West End Courier* was 25 cents, while a one-year subscription was $3.50.

The *West End Courier* differed from the *West Side Courier* only in its front page. "The guts of the paper were the same," recalled Ballard. "Phil (Hager) and I, as employees, saw immediately that this didn't work. You'd have your tea party in Shaughnessy (on the cover of) one paper and your prostitution problem in Vancouver's east end in the other. People could see that it was just a front page, and it failed."

In September of 1975, Lyndon Grove became the editor of the *West End Courier*. Grove, a former art and book review columnist, broadcaster, and advertising writer, had been a creative director of CHQM.

Others joining the staff of the *West End Courier* at that time included assistant editor Holly Botham, and photography director Nick Yunge-Bateman.

The *West End Courier* continued to publish until March of 1976. "They let the *West End Courier* just die," says Hager.

In contrast, the *West Side Courier* was thriving. Located in an office at 2140 West 12th Ave., the *West Side Courier* had expanded from its Kerrisdale roots to cover all of Vancouver's west side, including Shaughnessy, Dunbar, Point Grey, Kitsilano, West Broadway, South Granville, Arbutus Ridge, Oakridge/ Cambie, Marpole and the University area.

The weekly *West Side Courier* averaged 16 to 24 pages. The circulation was listed as 33,000. Cost of a single issue was 30 cents, while annual subscriptions were $6 if delivered by carrier, or $10 by mail.

Bill Forst, who had been with the newspaper prior to Lecky purchasing it, continued with the paper as its editor and assistant publisher, and Rod Raglin stayed on as advertising manager.

The newspaper continued to publish under the name *West Side Courier* for eight months. But by April of 1976, after the *West End Courier* had been abandoned, the name on the masthead was simply "the *Courier*" once more.

For many years, the paper had been published with a paid circulation of less than 20,000 subscribers. Lecky took it to controlled circulation (in which the number of papers printed is guaranteed and the paper is given away free of charge) and a "struggling" newspaper became a financial success.

"The five years that I was with the *Courier* were the best five years of the *Courier*'s life, both in terms of content and in terms of a growing advertising base," says Lecky. "Clearly it was being read."

First run of street car on Fourth Avenue, October 1909. City of Vancouver Archives, Kit. P. 24, N. 24.

Ballard recalled the newspaper as having a free circulation of about 40,000, plus a paid circulation of about 8,000. "(Paid circulation) was just an enormous waste of time and money, collecting two dollars here and two dollars there."

"We had a staff of two to three people in circulation," adds Hager.

During the 1970s, the competition on Vancouver's west side was the *Western News*. "It was about 12 pages an issue," says Hager. "It wasn't a factor. We loved having it there, because it kept out other papers."

"It's one thing to be the second paper in a burgeoning market," added Ballard. "But it's a whole different thing to be the third paper."

Dennis Gray-Grant published the *Western News*. "He was a very eccentric character," says Ballard.

"He ran the paper just so that he could write his editorial every week," added Hager. "The paper never made a bean."

"It was a classic romantic gesture," says Ballard. "We helped deliver it when he couldn't get it out because we knew his position was important to our position."

During the time that the *West End Courier* and *West Side Courier* were being published, the newspaper also expanded into West Vancouver.

"It was a natural (expansion)," says Ballard. "The west side, the West End, and West Vancouver. It had a nice linkage to it, similar demographics..."

"We lasted (in West Vancouver) about six weeks," says Ballard. "Peter Speck, (publisher) of the *North Shore News*, to this day has a 'kill or be killed' mentality."

"He didn't like us coming into his territory," adds Hager. "He sent in a sales person after every call we made who would go in and give the ad (in the *North Shore News*) away."

"We left with our tails between our legs in about six weeks, bruised and battered," says Ballard. "He really did kick us out of West Vancouver."

The late '70s were a time of rapid expansion for the *Courier*, both in terms of editorial content and advertising revenues. In 1979, as a result of an eight-month strike by Pacific Press (publisher of the *Sun* and *Province*) the *Courier* went daily. It was a short-lived venture; Pacific Press settled the strike just as the *Vancouver Courier* was launched. After just two months as a daily, the paper was forced into receivership and very nearly ceased to exist.

In the fall of 1979, what remained of the newspaper—its good will and back issues—was purchased by Peter Ballard, Phil Hager and Geoff Wellens, who had previously served as its sports editor. The trio formed a company known as Vancouver Courier (1979) Ltd. and re-launched the *Courier* in November of 1979 from an office at 6244 East Boulevard.

What made the newspaper work, says Wellens, was its informal, almost "family" atmosphere. Wellens, Hager and Ballard shared a similar disdain for business suits, and set the relaxed but professional atmosphere that prevails in the newspaper office to this day.

"We looked after our people, and paid them the same wages as the unionized people were getting," says Wellens. "So we never had any of our people wanting to bring in the unions. And we had the best Christmas parties and staff parties in the business."

As the 1970s drew to a close, the *Courier* began its rise from the ashes. Having come within a hair's breadth of ceasing to exist after its financially disastrous venture into the world of the dailies, it would work hard during the next decade to re-establish itself.

During the 1980s, the *Courier* changed its news format. Rather than running stories on crime, car crashes and fires—the sort of thing the daily newspapers could always get the "scoop" on—the community paper decided to focus on feature stories. The *Courier* billed itself "The Good News Paper."

By 1984, the newspaper had moved to 2094 West 43rd Avenue. Joy Jones was the assistant editor. That year, another strike hit Pacific Press. This time, it was of shorter duration – just two months – but it led to a windfall in advertising revenue for the *Courier*.

"We reacted immediately and boosted our circulation," says Phil Hager. "We went to two days a week, from 36 pages per week to 140 pages per week. We were prepared; we knew the strike was coming about a week before. So we were on the phones to all the agencies back east, and they started forwarding stuff before the strike was even called. We really reacted fast there, and in the two months we made as much money as (the *Courier*) did during the eight-month strike."

Having changed printers, the newspaper was no longer restricted to its 64-page limit, as it had been during the 1979 Pacific Press strike. Circulation was also boosted—rom 52,000 to 100,000. In addition to its regular west side edition, the newspaper added a Sunday edition that featured news, features, and TV listings. The "wraparound" city edition included provincial, national, and city news.

"There were lots of columns, and not much news," says Wellens. "There were all of the names that people were familiar with from the *Sun* and the *Province*." Denny Boyd wrote a piece for the dailies, and made the comment that the *Courier* had 'more columns than the parthenon.'"

Wellens (who retired in 1990) recalled the *Courier* as a friendly, informal place to work. Together with Ballard and Hager, he set a casual atmosphere – they scorned wearing suits to work, and jokingly formed a "fridge club" that met after work each day to consume the contents of a well stocked beer fridge.

Yet there was lots of hard work involved in building a successful

Last trip of the Observation Car on the B.C. Electric Railway, September 17, 1950. City of Vancouver Archives, Tran. P. 122, N. 123A.

community newspaper. A 16-hour day wasn't unusual. "We were working pretty hard," says Wellens. "At times, during the strike, we were putting out 140 pages."

All of the money made during the 1984 strike was plowed back into the business. The *Courier* finally moved to a larger office, and upgraded to a computerized newsroom. Before that, the newspaper had been put together with old fashioned cut-and-paste typesetting.

When the Pacific Press strike ended, the national advertisers returned to the dailies. The *Courier* returned to its once-a-week format.

In the meantime, the paper was facing a legal dispute, as a result of breaking its contract and going to a printer other than College. That dispute was settled out of court in 1984—ironically, as a result of revenues gained during the 1984 Pacific Press strike. Going with another printer and increasing the size of the paper had enabled the *Courier* to earn the advertising revenue it needed to settle the lawsuit.

Today, the *Courier* today is printed at Kodiak Press (owned by the same company that owns College Printers) despite the acrimony which used to exist between the two companies.

The *Courier* returned to a twice a week format in 1986, adding a Sunday edition that covered both the east and west sides of Vancouver. "We went very brash," says Hager. "We went out to 140,000 people, with full colour."

The circulation was subsequently reduced to its current level of 125,000 on Sundays and 60,000 on Wednesdays, the latter being an edition that was distributed only to Vancouver's west side. The Sunday paper was supported by revenue from the flyers it contained.

"If nothing else, we had a wrap to encase the flyers," says Ballard.

The 1990s would bring big changes to the newspaper that had started out as a four-page broadsheet, composed on a linotype and printed in the back shop. In the 1990s, rapidly evolving computer technologies allowed the *Courier* to adopt a new look as the paper was redesigned.

The 1990s also spelled an end to independent ownership of the paper.

The *Courier* had been independently owned since its inception, but the newspaper chains had started to show an interest in purchasing it as early as 1980.

Throughout the 1980s, various suitors came calling, offering to purchase the *Courier*. "We had offers that were quite substantial," says Ballard. "But we were pretty pumped. We were doing well and we wanted our independence."

"We were still in a growth pattern and weren't interested in selling, until Southam came to us with a serious offer," says Hager.

Eventually, in 1990, the offers became too good to refuse.

"What made it really obvious that it was the time to sell was that the two largest corporations in this area—Trinity International, producing the Metro Valley Group of papers, and Southam—were both at our door at the same time," says Ballard. "When you've got the two biggest guys in the game vying for your operation, there probably isn't a better time to sell."

Southam had come to Vancouver to negotiate the purchase of not just the *Courier*, but also two other community newspapers: the *North Shore News*, and the *Richmond Review*. Negotiations for the *Review* "turned sour," says Ballard, but the deal with the *North Shore News* went ahead. When it came time to negotiate for the *Courier*, Southam ultimately wound up with much more than it had bargained for.

A clause that dated back to the 1940s gave the owners of College Printers the right of first refusal to purchase the *Courier*. At that time, the owners of College also owned the Now Group of newspapers,

Kodiak Press, the *Real Estate Weekly* and Netmar Distribution. "They had been trying to shop that package to Southam for a number of years," says Ballard. "When Southam came to town to purchase us and realized that they couldn't have us without dealing with (College) they put a monster deal together. So instead of just getting two papers or three (newspapers), they ended up with 15 . . ."

". . . and two printing companies," adds Hager.

After months of negotiations, Southam purchased a 75 per cent share of the *Courier* on May 8, 1990 for $6 million. Hager and Ballard retained a 25 per cent interest, and were put on management contracts to run the paper. Wellens, 55 at the time of the purchase, retired.

In the years since the Southam purchase, the *Courier* has continued to evolve. The newspaper gained its current look in October of 1995. "We realized that we were getting 'old,'" says Ballard. "Our staff came to us and said, 'We don't read our own paper. We're younger than you, and we're not interested in it.'"

As a result, design director Peter Cocking, with help from staff, completely redesigned the paper. While the editorial content continues to focus on news that's closer to home, front-page cover stories are presented in a longer magazine-style format, a unique approach that has garnered the paper numerous awards and made the staff proud. The *Courier* looks forward to serving their community for another 90 years.

—Lisa Smedman

VANCOUVER ECHO

Although the *Echo* was founded in 1917, a framed 1922 four-page edition is the earliest known copy of the paper. Fire, the legend goes, destroyed virtually all file copies kept by the publisher in 1936.

But just prior to the 50th anniversary of the *Echo* in 1967, a single copy of the "Official Organ of the Grandview Chamber of Commerce" was found by Mr. and Mrs. Alfred Booker under the linoleum in their home. The Bookers had lived in Grandview since 1928.

The front page of the then-*Highland Echo* included editorializing

Leslie E. Barber, Chilliwack Progress.

on the morality of army conscription, Christian teachings on the pampering of pets in a time when children go to bed hungry and pre-set filler items like "Keep your pants pressed and your shoes shined."

Top news stories included the return of Mrs. Chas. E. Smith and daughter Mlle. Yvonne Dongelzer from a tour of the Old Country and France and the opening of a branch store by renowned baker J.

H. Adams making it possible for Grandview residents to procure a block cake without travelling into town.

The McComber Bros. shop at 1513 Commercial Drive offered for sale local creamery butter at 43 cents per pound and eggs at 36 for $1.15 according to the front-page advertisement.

But it was technology that put the Highland in the *Echo*—cutting edge telephone technology gave the *Echo* its original name. Originally dubbed the *Highland Echo* by founder Mark C. Gilchrist, the name was coined from the Highland telephone exchange, which served Grandview in 1917.

Although the exchange changed from Highland to Hastings to Alpine before prefixes turned numeric, no publisher had the heart to change the name until Jack Burch came along. He changed the flag to *Vancouver Echo* to reflect broader circulation and the end of Grandview's physical and spiritual isolation from the other neighbourhoods of Vancouver.

The *Echo* has been an East Vancouver institution since 1917.

As for the *Echo's* founder and original publisher Mark C. Gilchrist, clippings and vague remembrances are all that remain of his legacy.

A dashing 27-year-old draped with a cape and punctuated with a top hat and cane, Gilchrist operated the newspaper from an executive office at 1830 Commercial Drive, a publication office at 319 Broadway East and a city office at far away 525 Richards Street. Little is known of Gilchrist's other business ventures although they must have been substantial.

Gilchrist sold the *Echo* in 1921 and went on to work and earn a pension as a bookkeeper in an unknown locale until his retirement in Los Angeles. A partly destroyed 1958 newspaper clipping from *Los Angeles' Mirror News* describes Gilchrist's charity work.

Then 68 years old, the former newspaper publisher spent his days sewing dresses with an old-style treadle sewing machine, wrote the *Mirror News*. Financing the work from his pension, Gilchrist sent the clothing to children overseas who had been abandoned by their American servicemen fathers.

Under the headline "Bachelor sews for unloved tots," the article quotes Gilchrist, "And I intend to keep the work up as long as I have a dollar to my name." He died a few years later in his early 70s.

Alex "A. G." Holmes followed Gilchrist as the paper's owner. He

was one of Commercial
Drive's leading citizens
during his three dec-
ades as publisher of the
Echo. A.G. was a veteran
of South Africa's Boer
War, which ended in
1902. He remained in
South Africa as opera-
tor of a newspaper plant
before working for
newspapers in Toronto
and Detroit and week-
lies across the Canadian
Prairies before arriving
in Vancouver.

BCYCNA Board, 1997.

Holmes hired then
26-YEAR-OLD Jack
Burch as an assistant
and advertising salesman in 1948. A Royal Canadian Air Force veteran and holder of the Distinguished Flying Cross, Burch went to
work for the generous sum of $35 per week. Burch would later buy in
to the company as a partner and then full owner when Holmes retired
in 1955.

During his career Holmes was a charter member of the Vancouver
East Lions and a secretary of the Grandview Chamber of Commerce.

Recalled Jack Burch, "A friend and advisor to all who knew him,
Mr. Holmes was acknowledged as one of the leaders in this community throughout all his long stay."

The *Echo* had occupied offices up and down Commercial Drive
over the years. But by 1955 when Burch assumed the helm, the newspaper was sharing space with Grandview Printing at 1464 Commercial Drive. In the fall of 1957 the two companies combined forces.
The new Grandview Printing and Publishing Company moved into a
vacated sheet metal shop at 1720 Graveley Street just a few yards
from Commercial Drive.

Hilarious typographical errors are part of the lore of every newsroom, but in 1965 editor Jack Burch let one slip through that tops them all.

The *Echo* had followed the life events of a certain local woman widely known the in the church community noticing her graduation, marriage and eventually her demise. Unfortunately a typo in the death announcement caused an enormous uproar, the cancellation of subscriptions and several advertisers to withdraw their ads.

The following week Burch dedicated the *Echo's* editorial space to an explanation of the mistake written in mock King James English. The following is an excerpt:

All flesh is grass and in time the wife is gathered into the silo. The minister getteth his bit. The editor printeth a death notice, two columns of obituary, three lodge notices, a cubit of poetry, and a card of thanks. And he forgetteth to read proof on the head, and the darn thing cometh out "Gone to Her Last Roasting Place." And all that are akin to the deceased jumpeth on the editor with exceeding great jumps. And they pulleth their ads and cancelleth their subscriptions and they swing the hammer until the third and fourth generations.

All things considered, circulation continued to grow and in the 1980s a second Hastings East edition of the *Echo* had long outstripped the company's ability to print in-house. Preparations began to split the printing and newspaper portions of the business again.

The *Echo* meantime continued to expand its circulation area and in 1988 hired its first fulltime editor, Randy Shore, after the departure of eight-year veteran reporter Nancy Suzuki. In just 75 years, the Grandview-area newspaper grew from a few hundred copies to a peak circulation of 63,000 by the mid-1990s.

—*Randy Shore*

VANCOUVER, WEST END TIMES

 The *West End Times* was founded in September 1990 by Bruce and Gail Coney.

Having emigrated from South Africa in 1982, Bruce Coney went to work for the *West Ender* newspaper. Starting out as a sales rep, his community newspaper knowledge and experience, natural ability and an extremely hard-working attitude soon resulted in quick promotions to sales manager and later to sales director in charge of advertising.

Coney played an integral part in the launch of the *East Ender* newspaper in 1993.

When the *West Ender* was sold to the Metro Valley Newspaper Group, Coney became the general manager. After spending some time in that position, he decided it was time to make some big changes to his career—from staff member to entrepreneur.

In September 1990, Bruce and Gail Coney, with financial assistance from Peter Walton, launched the *West End Times*. With a circulation of 16,000 in its first edition, the new paper began a competition with the *West Ender* that continues to this day.

In 1994 the *West End Times* joined forces with the Vancouver Area Newspaper Network and became the group's West End and downtown newspaper. At the same time through a unique joint venture, the *West End Times* and the *Real Estate Weekly* organization launched the West End edition of the *Real Estate Weekly*. Circulation of the *West End Times* increased to 25,000.

Today the *West End Times* is proud to serve its area and will continue to report news that's worth reading.

VANCOUVER, WEST ENDER

The *West Ender* debuted on July 12, 1951 as a community newspaper devoted "to the interest of the West End its organizations, its business enterprises and its people."

The original owner of the *West Ender*, which served a geographic neighbourhood that roughly covered the downtown peninsula in the City of Vancouver, was Abe Arnold. But Fred Lyle, who was initially hired as an advertising salesman, became publisher and editor by the third issue. Working with his wife Elaine, the Lyles went on to run the newspaper for the next two decades until the fall of 1970.

Originally published twice a month, the *West Ender* began publishing weekly in 1955. In those early days, the cost of an annual subscription was $1 a year and advertising sold for 75 cents a column inch.

West Ender editor Ted Townsend (left) and Advertising Manager Leslie Shtabsky (second from left) present a piano to Judi Angel and Staci McDonald of the Dr. Peter Centre, a hospice and daycare centre for persons living with AIDS. The piano was purchased with funds raised through a special editorial/advertising supplement in 1997.

Competition was fierce, Lyle remembered in a 1984 profile, but the *West Ender* succeeded by sticking to basics: "Every community had its own newspaper then, with eight, 10, 12 pages. We stayed with our community. I've always had a definite idea what a community paper should do. It should give space to current MPS and MLAS, even city council in every paper."

Lyle, who remained a West End resident until his death in the early 1990s, was proudest of his newspaper role in promoting the establishment of several seniors' housing projects in the West End.

In the 1970s,the *West Ender* had a variety of owners, most notably Thomas Kelly, before it was purchased by cross-town competitor the *Vancouver Courier* in July 1975.

The *Courier* briefly published the *West Ender* under its own name, before renaming it the *West End Courier* in August 1975. That publication lasted only a few months before being closed in March of 1976.

Three years later the *West Ender* was reborn. Backed by Buy and Sell Press publisher Mike Abbott, the new *West Ender* published its

Photo by Bonny Makarewicz, Whistler Question.

first edition on July 12, 1979. It reunited many of the key players from the newspaper's previous incarnation, including managing editor Jack Moore, advertising manager Doug Dulmage, contributing editors Kevin McKeown (who would later become managing editor) and Bob Cummings and photographer Franco Citarelli.

Moore promised the new *West Ender* would be a community resource: "That, after all, is what community newspapers are all about"

During the 1980s, the *West Ender* played a major role in promoting the "Shame The Johns" movement, which eventually succeeded in pushing street prostitution out of West End neighbourhoods.

The *West Ender* was sold to the Metro Valley Newspaper Group in January of 1990. Metro Valley is a chain of community newspapers, stretching from Hope to Bowen Island, which at the time was owned by the Liverpool-based Trinity Holdings.

Under Metro Valley ownership the newspaper has continued to grow and thrive. Early in 1990 Ken Wood became publisher of the *West Ender*, while Ted Townsend was appointed as editor.

Under the new leadership, the *West Ender* made significant investments in editorial quality, production standards and computers.

With additional staff and an increased commitment to editorial, the newspaper has won several dozen national and provincial journalism awards in recent years, including national first-place awards for feature writing and photography.

A strong commitment to serving the community has also continued and the *West Ender* has twice been a top-three finalist for the Canadian Community Newspapers Association's community service award.

Over the past decade, the *West Ender* has had a number of offshoots including the *East Ender* and *Vancouver News* (serving East Vancouver) and the *Kitsilano News*.

A new leaf was turned over at the start of 1997, when Metro Valley Newspaper Group, including the *West Ender*, was purchased by well-known B.C. newspaperman David Black.

In early 1997, a new era of growth began as are designed and refocused *West Ender* was launched as "Vancouver's urban voice."

Currently the *West Ender* has a weekly free distribution of 43,000 and serves a number of Vancouver neighbourhoods including the West End, Yaletown and Kitsilano.

WHISTLER QUESTION

 "I'm a newshound, always have been, always will be," says Paul Burrows, founder of the *Whistler Question*.

In 1976, Burrows was looking for a new career. His unsuccessful attempt to become Whistler's first mayor had given him pause. But what to do?

"My wife and I looked around Whistler and thought: what does

Photo by Paul Andrew, Whistler Question.

this place need?" he says. "It came down to starting a bus company or a newspaper. We picked newspaper because it was a cheaper business venture."

With the most primitive equipment possible, Burrows started pro-

Photo by Bonnie Makarewicz, Whistler Question.

ducing the *Question* out of the basement of his home.

"It looked nothing like what a newspaper was supposed to look like, but the content was great," he admits proudly. "We even won a couple of awards for our work."

The four-page, mime-
ographed newspaper,
with a circulation of 200,
was lapped up by local
residents. Within a year
the paper had expanded
and became a tabloid
weekly.

Finding stories to do
was never a problem for
Burrows, it was making
sure they were done
fairly and accurately.

Whister Question *typist Pat Hocking and Assistant
to the Editor, Brad Cooper, August 1978.*

"Some really diverse people live in this area. If you slip up or show
bias, all hell breaks loose."

Burrows believes that attitude remains in Whistler.

"Everybody in this town thinks they have the answers to everything here," he says. "That's a real challenge for a newpaper because
you will never please everybody and that can be frustrating."

Burrows sold the paper in 1982 to his then editor, Glenda Bartosh.
She sold it one year later to Bob Doull, who at the time was buying up
papers across B.C. and Alberta. Doull's chain of papers in B.C. and
Alberta, Westmount Press Ltd., was sold in 1998 to Bowes Publishers, a division of Sun Media Corporation based in London, Ontario.
Along with the *Squamish Chief* and the *Bridge River-Lillooet News*, the
Question was then sold again to Lower Mainland Publishing, who in
turn sold it to Madison Holdings Ltd.. In August 1998, Penny Graham, publisher of the *Squamish Chief*, took on the publishing duties of
the *Question*. She brought with her the *Chief's* editor, Al Price, a veteran of 25 years in the community newspaper business.

And Paul Burrows? He is still a faithful columnist for the *Question*,
ruffling the feathers of council and poking fun at some extremely serious issues. Some *Whistler Question* reporters and editors wonder if
Burrows thinks he still holds his title as editor and publisher.

"Every now and then, I get the old, red pen out and start circling
typos and editorial inconsistencies," he says with a grin. "Then I call
the paper and tell them."

"What can I say, I just can't stop myself."

WHITE ROCK, PEACE ARCH NEWS

The *Peace Arch News*, founded in 1976 by printer Roy Jelly, has earned itself a reputation as a newspaper with heart, giving thousands of dollars to improve the quality of living in the community in which it serves. The White Rock-South Surrey newspaper has always done its share to support worthwhile community organizations and charitable causes.

Eleven years ago, the paper created the *Peace Arch News* Christmas Fund, which raises donations for valued groups and money for needy families. Each year, the *News* publishes a series of stories sharing needy groups' and families' stories with sympathetic readers. The paper also holds an annual wine/auction evening called Vintage Affair. In 1997, the paper broke its record, raising more than $60,000.

The *News* has come a long way from its humble beginnings. The first issue of the *Peace Arch News* and *Consumer's Guide* was published on February 10, 1976, landing on 13,000 doorsteps on the Semiahmoo Peninsula. Its founder, Roy Jelly, wore a number of hats including publisher, editor, ad salesman, photographer, make-up artist and delivery boy for the new paper in town. As there were only two "stringers," Jelly did nearly everything himself.

But as the paper grew, so did the staff. And the *Peace Arch News* became the paper of record as its only competitor, the *White Rock Sun*, folded in 1982. Now the paper has a staff of more than 60 and reaches 30,000 households and publishes an average of 100 pages a week, plus many special sections. Jelly finally retired in 1985 at the age of 64, but looks back on his years at the *Peace Arch News* as one of the most exciting times in his life.

The *News* continues to keep up at an exciting pace, introducing new products and improving established ones. New sections include a seven-issue golf section *Tee Times*, a bi-monthly car section called *Wheels* and a *Westcoast Lifestyle Magazine* which is delivered around the peninsula as well as Ladner and Tsawwassen. Established products continue to flourish, including the *News'* annual *Summer Guide*, which has been the biggest in Canada for several years running.

One of the greatest strengths of the *Peace Arch News* is its editorial coverage. The paper's editorial team wins awards every year for everything from photography to editorials, columns, news stories, features and stories that recognize volunteer efforts. The White Rock-South Surrey paper has been ranked one of the top newspapers in its class in B.C. and Yukon many times and continues to enjoy a healthy share of the area's readership. Now that's a good place to be.

Southern Interior

NORTH THOMPSON

The Times

REVELSTOKE
TIMES REVIEW

PEACHLAND
Signal

OSOYOOS TIMES
Volume 53 - Number 2   Wednesday, January 13, 1999

SUMMERLAND Review

Armstrong Advertiser

In the ever-evolving landscape of the B.C. and Yukon newspaper industry, some things haven't changed: since August 1927 the *Armstrong Advertiser* and the Jamieson family have been synonymous.

Ed. V. Chambers established the *Armstrong Advertiser* in May 1902 and the first issue hit the streets on May 15. Chambers sold the paper 18 short months later to the Vernon News Printing and Publishing Company but continued as business manager. For 20 years following that, the newspaper was bought and sold by Samuel Polson, Norman Cary, E.V. Chambers again, then to Norman Cary and his brother Sidney and in 1924 to Frank Briscoe. Finally, in 1927, a man named John E. Jamieson bought the paper and stability was reached.

"I do this because I love it," says Jack Jamieson, the most recent family member to act as publisher of the paper. "My dad actually tried to dissuade me from entering the business, but once I got a taste of it there was no stopping me."

John E. Jamieson operated the paper until his death in 1954. John M. Jamieson and his brother James operated the business together until they sold it to John M.'s son, Jack, in 1969.

"I wanted to be a fisheries biologist," admits Jack Jamieson. It was a short-term move back home that changed his mind. Working for his dad at the newspaper, young Jack let the "ink seep into his veins." Before anyone knew it, he switched his major and was attending journalism school.

Eventually, after working as a reporter and editor, Jack Jamieson decided to buy his own newspaper. Just when he thought he had found the perfect publication, he phoned his dad to tell him the good news.

"That's when I learned Dad and Uncle Jim were selling the *Advertiser*," says Jamieson. "So I bought it."

Thirty years later, Jack Jamieson remains publisher and owner of the *Armstrong Advertiser*. But he may be the last Jamieson in a long line.

"My two kids are not interested," he says. "And I'm fine with that—really."

Whether or not his kids will let any ink seep into their veins has yet to be determined. But as it stands now, the *Armstrong Advertiser* and the Jamieson family are still one and the same.

ASHCROFT-CACHE CREEK JOURNAL

 The *Ashcroft-Cache Creek Journal* celebrated its 100th birthday May 9, 1995.

It was first published on May 9, 1895, making it one of the oldest continuous operating weekly newspapers in the province. Dr. F.S. Reynolds and A.H.S. Sroufe founded the paper under the name of the *B.C. Mining Journal* but left the business about a year later. Dr. Reynolds changed the name to the *Ashcroft Journal* in 1899 and continued to operate it for three more years. Then from 1902 until 1908 J.E. Knight was the owner until he sold to D.W. Rowlands, the publisher from 1908 to 1912. In June that year R.D. Cummings bought the *Journal* from Rowlands and the paper was in the Cummings family continuously until 1978.

Townspeople from Ashcroft and surrounding area enjoy the 100th birthday party on the lawn at the Journal. *The old building, built in 1916, has survived three major fires which destroyed most of downtown Ashcroft on each occasion.*

R.D. Cummings was the man in charge for 23 years until ill health forced him to retire in 1935. He was followed by his two sons: T.A. Cummings ran the enterprise from 1935 to 1944 and L.W. Cummings took over from 1944-1958. His son, L.E. Cummings, took over from him in 1958 and remained publisher until the paper was sold to Cariboo Press on October 1, 1978.

The community of Ashcroft was established during the period when miners were following the gold trail from the lower Fraser. Then the CPR rail line came through, reaching for the coast, and Ashcroft became the railhead to the Cariboo gold fields.

Only two other papers in B.C. have longer records of continuous operation and the *Ashcroft Journal* has a complete set of files from 1895 to the present day to show for it.

Still owned by Cariboo Press, and going into its second 100 years, the award-winning *Journal* continues to serve the Interior communities of Lytton, Spences Bridge, Logan Lake, Ashcroft, Cache Creek, Clinton, Walhachin and Savona and the rural areas in between.

BARRIERE, NORTH THOMPSON STAR JOURNAL

 The *North Thompson Star Journal* traces its origins to 1974, when Barriere's first newspaper began publication.

A 12-page tabloid, stapled together and printed on yellow bond paper, it was called the *Barriere Bulletin*, and was published on alternate Thursdays at a subscription cost of $7 per year. The publishers were George Haskins and his son Ward.

Michael Gardner and his mother, Ita, took the paper over in 1980 or 1981 and changed its name to the *North Thompson Journal* in May of 1981 before handing the reins to his sister, Wendy Gardner, later that year.

In 1986 Vern Monson of Kamloops purchased the paper. Monson opened a second office, at Clearwater, in 1988. Then, in 1990, Monson sold the operation to Tim and Janice Francis soon after they purchased the Barriere-based *Thompson Advertiser* from Darcy Hadden. The *Advertiser*, as it changed hands, became the *Yellowhead Star*.

Two publications were produced from a main Barriere office and a

North Thompson Star Journal. *Photo by Ann Piper.*

Clearwater satellite office, with the *Journal* tailored for the Clearwater/North Valley market and the *Yellowhead Star* serving the needs of the southern sections of the valley, from Heffley Creek to Little Fort.

The *North Thompson Journal* and the *Yellowhead Star* were combined to become the *North Thompson Star Journal* in November 1993. In August 1994, Tim and Janice Francis sold the *Star Journal* to Cariboo Press.

In October 1997, Cariboo Press purchased the *Star Journal's* competitor, the Clearwater-based *North Thompson Times*. The valley was again divided into two readership areas. The *Times* now serves the valley from Little Fort to Blue River, while the *Star Journal* covers communities from Heffley Creek to Little Fort.

The *Star Journal* and the *Times* now share a single production department at the *Star Journal's* Barriere offices, with separate editorial departments, but share news of interest to the valley as a whole.

CLEARWATER, NORTH THOMPSON TIMES

The North Thompson Times is based in Clearwater, a small community of approximately 2,000 people (8,500 in the North Thompson area) located 120 km north of Kamloops along the highway to Jasper. The economy of the area is primarily forestry-based, but tourism is gaining more and more importance. A major attraction is nearby Wells Gray Park and its world famous Helmcken Falls.

The first issue of the *Times* came out on September 23, 1964. Owner, publisher and editor was David Berryman. Originally from Saskatchewan, his family had moved to the Okanagan in 1959.

In 1969 Berryman acquired a partner, Frank Tonge, originally from Manchester, England. A linotype operator by trade, he had worked for numerous newspapers across the province, including the *Vancouver Sun* and the *Vancouver Province*. For the first year Tonge commuted weekly from Salmon Arm to Clearwater. In 1970 his wife, Christena, and their five children joined him in the North Thompson. Christena was a Nova Scotian by birth, but had spent her childhood on the Sunshine Coast. She and Frank had met while he was working at the *Sun*.

In 1974 ill health forced Berryman to sell his share of the business to Len Sonneson. Sonneson had come to Clearwater from Seattle to join the *Times*, but after a year or two he went to work for a local lum-

Programme

Nineteenth
Annual Convention

CANADIAN WEEKLY
NEWSPAPERS ASSOCIATION

VANCOUVER
August 11th, 12th & 13th
1 9 3 8

ber company, Clearwater Timber Products.

For the first 13 years the *Times* was produced in true pioneer style. The owners and their helpers printed, folded and assembled each weekly issue themselves. Power fluctuations caused by a nearby sawmill led to problems with their Linotype parts, which had to be repaired or replaced by local welders. Saw filers from the planer mill were called on to repair nicks in the paper cutter blades.

The newspaper was constructed two metal pages at a time. Weighing over 200 pounds, they were carried to an adjacent shed, which held the press. In winter an old wood stove was used to heat the shed. Frank Tonge recalled that in extreme conditions the stove's chimney might be glowing red, while the pressman was dressed like an Eskimo as he kept an eye on the 1,000-plus run.

In 1975 they purchased their first computer, a Compugraphic, which was a major step forward in speed and accuracy. Two years later, in 1977, printing of the *Times* was contracted out to the *Kamloops Daily News*. Frank contrasted the new arrangement with their earlier struggles. Now he could drop the flats off, go out for a cup of coffee, and the newspaper would be printed when he came back.

Around 1987 production switched to desktop publishing using computers. At about this time two of the Tonges' sons, Darren and David, joined the *Times* for several years, then moved on to other endeavours. During this period the paper won several awards, including second best front page across Canada in its class.

After almost 24 years under the Tonges' control, the *Times* was sold in March of 1993 to Nancy and Bruce Chappell. Nancy was former managing editor of the *Nelson Daily News*, while her husband, Bruce, had been a car salesman in Castlegar.

In September 1997 the Chappells sold the *Times* to George Manning of Small Town Press Ltd.. Manning in turn sold it almost immediately to its present owners, Cariboo Press, a chain of Interior newspapers headquartered in Williams Lake. The newspaper chain already owned the *Star-Journal* in the neighbouring community of Barriere. Carol Gardarsson, publisher of the *Star-Journal*, became the *Times'* publisher as well. Lee Toop, a reporter when the Chappells owned the newspaper, became *Times* editor. Early in 1998 Toop left to work in Merritt. Keith McNeil, who had worked as reporter/photographer and assistant editor for the Tonges for 10 years, took his place as editor.

The *Times* continues to be a subscription-based community newspaper. Date of publication is Monday of each week and the geographic area covered is the North Thompson valley from Little Fort in the south to Blue River in the north.

ENDERBY COMMONER

Henry Milton Walker was born in Simcoe County, Ontario, in 1871 and learned the printing trade while living in California. He came north to British Columbia and into the Kootenays where the lure of gold had led his father in 1890.

He worked with Col. Lowery in several of the early mining towns and then moved to Vancouver to work on the former daily, the *News-Advertiser*.

The Okanagan lured him back in 1904 when he went to Enderby and established the *Edenograph*. Things didn't go well and he returned to California for a couple of years, returning to Enderby in 1908 where he started *Walker's Weekly*.

During World War I, the *Armstrong Advertiser* and the Enderby paper were amalgamated into the *Okanagan Commoner*. At the end of the war the two papers went their separate ways again and *Walker's Weekly* became the *Enderby Commoner*.

Today Enderby residents continue to enjoy the *Commoner*, although now it is closely tied with the *Salmon Arm*, *Shuswap Sun* and publisher Robin Campbell.

THE GOLDEN STAR

The Golden Star has been serving the community of Golden since 1891. When it was established at the time under publisher E.A. Haggen, the paper was known as *The Golden Era*. Haggen was a mining engineer who came to Golden from Australia. He sold the paper to another mining company in 1903, and shortly thereafter, the paper was renamed *The Golden Star*.

In 1906, the paper was sold again to H.G. Parson, a local merchant. After Parson's death Wilbur Fish acquired *The Star*. Wilbur's son Denny eventually took over operation of the paper and, in 1969 sold *The Star* to Herb Hilderbrand.

The paper changed ownership numerous times throughout the late 70s and early 80s as local would-be newspaper barons attempted to seize control of the competitive market in Golden.

The Star was eventually acquired by WestMount Press Limited, based in Cochrane, Alberta, in 1987. On a more recent note, West-Mount was acquired by Bowes Publishing Limited, in April 1998.

Throughout the years, *The Star* has not been without some colourful publishers and editors. While most of the editors kept themselves in check, some publishers loved nothing more than a good, old-fashioned, newspaper war with the paper down the street.

Julia Cundliffe and Holly Magoon are just two of the more recent publishers who enjoyed rolling up their sleeves. Their little scraps with notorious Golden newspaperman Duane Crandall are legendary. Current editor Roger Smith has kept the tradition alive—and Crandall on his toes.

The Star takes its role very seriously and is looking forward to continuing to do so into the new millennium.

GRAND FORKS GAZETTE

It was not easy bringing out a newspaper in the days before computers. During the winter of 1896-1897 when the *Grand Forks Gazette* was an infant, deep snow crippled the Boundary area. It was impossible to get supplies in from the Okanagan or from Spokane.

Incorporated in 1897, the paper was owned, operated and printed by F.H. McCarter & Sons. That winter they were forced to work in a cold canvas tent, a rag dipped in bacon grease for light, and hand peg the type. There was no newsprint to use so they recycled wrapping paper.

The next week the paper came out on wallpaper.

Collecting money was difficult for early publishers, too. In the early days cash was in short supply, payment sometimes was in poker chips or a good cigar, or a chicken for Sunday dinner. If a customer did not pay his bill, his ad was printed upside down!

The first issue of the *Grand Forks Gazette* under the new owners, Senator R.F. Greene, Donald McCallum, Martin Burrell, and Charles Pearson (printer), was published April 8, 1905 with Martin Burrell as editor and Donald McCallum as business manager.

Martin Burrell soon became sole owner of the paper but his interest in politics started taking over when he was elected mayor in 1903. In 1908 he became an MP and distinguished himself by closing the steel doors connecting the Parliamentary Library with the east wing when fire broke out. This simple move helped prevent the fire from spreading to the priceless collection of books and manuscripts. He was a true Canadian hero.

By January 1911, it became evident that politics, not newspapering, was taking all of Martin Burrell's attention. T.A. Love came down from Phoenix to help and ended up buying the paper. Thomas (Tommy) Love would serve 13 terms as mayor of Grand Forks as well as serving as a Conservative His reporting covered two world wars, the Depression, bootlegging and air travel. Love bought the first Linotype in 1917, publishing the first machine-composition paper. Made by Canadian Linotype Ltd., it set lines of type of a wide range of width from four to 30 centimetres. Stanley Orris, affectionately known as Old Moe, bought the *Gazette* in January 1943. Writing in

Bruce Winfield accepts second prize for editorial writing at the BCYNA Convention in September 1981.

his column *The Orriscope*, he recalled buying the *Gazette*, on a cash basis, with a guaranteed circulation of 1,200. An audit a month later showed the actual paid circulation of 549. One of the many excuses he heard for people not paying was: "Oh, I never pay for the paper. Mr. Love said that if I voted for him then he would send me the paper for free!"

Stanley Orris was known for his love of books, and sold books and stationery from the front of the *Gazette*. Not only did he run the newspaper, but also he actively promoted the town, serving as national president of the Board of Trade.

He was awarded the Freedom of the City in July 1979 and the Grand Forks and District Public Library is housed in the Stanley Orris building.

Under his guidance, the *Gazette* actively encouraged local contributors to submit poetry and original manuscripts.

In 1973 it published "Rut Hog or Die" by Sylvia Bannert. Orris was always willing to loan books from his extensive library. He also helped edit and publish Boundary Historical Society books.

Attendees to the BCYCNA Convention (1981), left to right: Fred Arthurs, Adelaide Black, Alan Black, Dawn Smith, John Smith.

Often the whole family helped to get the paper out. Mrs. Orris and the two children, Milton and Dawn, all helped. Milton wrote a column called "Young Moe," and set type when the typesetter went on vacation.

Over the years, staff have been expected to become part of the *Gazette's* family, going on fishing and hunting trips, on excursions to Lynch Creek and Ward's Lake. If there was a ball game or a hockey match, often the printer and typesetter were part of the team.

Once the entire staff was badly upset when the wagon they were in overturned on the way home from a weekend picking huckleberries at Christina Lake. Blankets, baby, pots and pans went flying, but the editor had sense enough to grab the buckets of berries.

In 1971, the paper was sold but the Orris family was forced to take it back again. Son Milton served as editor before going east. In the summer of 1974 John Smith joined the *Gazette* and took over as publisher in January 1975. He introduced the first TV guide, as well as excellent sports coverage.

Editors since Mr. Orris have been Earl Dunlop, Dave Butler, Jackie Pleasants, Mike Hogan, Alec Tully, Darcy Chernysh, Terry Arseneau, Mia Thomas and Richard Finnigan.

On December 1, 1992, The Gazette Publishing Company was sold to Sterling Newspapers Ltd.. In February 1996, Sandra Watts became publisher when John Smith was promoted to West Kootenay Regional Manager for Sterling, moving to Nelson.

The *Gazette* continues to be the Voice of the Fabulous Boundary Country.

—*R.S. Simbrec*

GREENWOOD, BOUNDARY CREEK TIMES

 Reed Turcotte is not 100 years old but some days, when the busy life of a new publisher gets to him, he feels it.

The *Boundary Creek Times* was founded in 1896, making it more than 100. Turcotte did not arrive on the scene until December 1997 when he bought the paper from Richard and Joyce Furness who had owned the little paper that could for three years.

His purchase also included the building, a modest and incredibly tiny space in downtown Greenwood that also functions as printing and publishing company.

Boundary Creek Times, *1998.*

INVERMERE, THE VALLEY ECHO

The history of the newspapers in the Windermere Valley could fill a book. *The Valley Echo* is the only one that has survived the trials and tribulations of the years.

The Valley Echo had six predecessors: *The Canterbury Outcrop*, *The Wilmer Outcrop*, the *Columbian*, the *Columbia Valley Times*, *The Valley News* and the *Columbia Valley Echo*.

The first newspaper in the Invermere area was called *The Canterbury Outcrop*, which was published in 1900 by Edward Mulholland and his assistant E. Evans. This publication survived until February of 1903 when Evans left town. There was not another newspaper until August 1911, when the first issue of the *Columbia* was published, but due to a lack of patronage, it lasted only until January 1912. The editor was J.A. McDougall, who was assisted by James Butterfield. In February 1913, the *Columbia Valley Times* appeared, which was instigated by W.H. Cleland.

The Columbia Valley news started publication under P.L. Conroy and John McLeod in 1954. It was sold to Earl Gray in 1955. In 1956, it was sold again to three Calgary businessmen, including F.B. Conduit, and received the name *The Lake Windermere Valley Echo*.

The new owners purchased the mailing list of the defunct valley paper for $50. The entire operation was run from a corner of editor Winnifred Weir's kitchen. The 48x60-inch space housed a typewriter, telephone, an apple box filing cabinet and a calendar.

Winnifred Weir still talks about typing out the editorial with one hand, while stirring soup with the other.

At that time, copy was being sent to Calgary by bus for printing, but in 1957, the printing was moved to Kimberley. Then in 1958 printing machinery was brought to Invermere, and the newspaper was moved to a brick building, which was formerly a Chinese laundry. Ron Ede moved from Kimberley to act as manager of the paper. Approximately six years later, Ron hired his wife Isabelle to run the press, and then in 1974 Isabelle took over as editor.

In 1965, it moved to its present location in downtown Invermere. The back office was opened up in order to house the press equipment.

In 1975, Ron and Isabelle Ede purchased the newspaper, which

The newly-formed Ultimate Leage in Kamloops. Photo by Brendan Harper. Kamloops This Week.

they successfully ran for 13 years. It soon became a true family business—daughter Deb working in production and son Bob running the press. In 1986, both Ron and Isabelle Ede received the CCNA Silver Quill award for their contributions to weekly newspapers.

In January of 1988 WestMount Press Limited purchased *The Valley Echo*. After a sewer flood in June 1996, the building received a very well deserved renovation, both inside and out. In May 1998, it again changed hands. It is now owned by Bowes Publishers Limited. Winnifred Weir, who is now 89 years of age, was editor from 1956 to 1974 and still writes a weekly column.

The Valley Echo boasts a circulation of 3,500, serving a population of approximately 8,000, including the communities of Invermere, Windermere, Wilmer, Fairmont Hot Springs and Radium Hot

Springs. It is located in the heart of the Rockies, a mere three-hour drive from Calgary.

KAMLOOPS THIS WEEK

 In 10 years *Kamloops This Week* has emerged from the ashes of the *Super Shopper*. Since Cariboo Press purchased the weekly, full-colour advertiser in September 1988, it has grown to a tri-weekly newspaper.

"Each time the paper grew it was on the basis of demand," says Cariboo Press vice-president Don Moores, who joined *KTW* as advertising manager in 1989.

"We were looking at between 88 and 112 pages a week and the readers and advertisers really enjoyed it."

Publisher Linda Hooton, recently named woman of the year by the Business and Professional Women's Club of Kamloops, is just one of the many award winners on *KTW* staff. Also in the ranks of the recognized are members of the editorial and photography staff, including editor Ken Alexander, as well as creative advertising design consultants.

KTW is also one of the first places people in the community call when they are hosting an event, announcing a new development or simply acknowledging a special person. At the same time, *KTW's* four news and community writers, two sports scribes and two photographers search for stories in every corner of the city – dedicated to bringing the best and most original stories to Kamloops . . . this week.

KELOWNA CAPITAL NEWS

The *Kelowna Capital News* began as a family operation and that thread continues to this day.

"My father-in-law (Les Kerry) started it in 1930," recalls former publisher Graham Takoff. "It was a one-page lithograph originally. It was published weekly."

Takoff came on board as a full-time employee in 1960 and rolled up his sleeves and went to work.

A young Kamloops boy enjoys the Riverside Park water park. Photo by Jason Payne, Kamloops This Week.

"I started as an ad salesman/reporter," says Takoff. "I guess you could say I've done it all."

During Takoff's tenure the paper went from weekly to three times a week.

"It (expansion) was the thing to do back then," says Takoff. "By going three times a week you could make more money."

In 1968, Takoff and his wife Jane bought the *Capital News* from Kerry and he was the publisher until 1986 when he sold to the Lower Mainland Publishing Limited group.

"The highlight during the 33 years I was with the *Capital News* was coming to work every day," says Takoff. "Every day was different. Boy, we had some characters over the years, but we won't get into that. We worked hard but boy, we had a lot of fun, too."

Kerry's grandson, Graham's son Brian, carries on the family tradition, working in the pressroom of the *Capital News* today.

"I started in 1981 in the classified ad department," recalls Brian. "I got out of school in 1977 and I worked horseshoeing for four years. Then, in 1982 I think it was, a flyboy quit so I moved into the press room and I've been there ever since."

Today, Brian is a colour stripper and platemaker.

One can hear the pride in his voice as he talks about his father.

"Yeah, Dad did everything," says Brian. "I believe he was the editor for a while and sometimes he even ran the press. In the late 60s they installed a four-unit press and that really changed everything."

The Kelowna Capital News continues to grow and change, always ready to meet the challenges the future holds.

—*Al Paterson*

MERRITT HERALD

Rich coal deposits gave the City of Merritt its first boom in 1908 and resulted in the establishment of the *Merritt Herald*. Prior to this period, a newspaper had been printed since May 18, 1905, called the *Nicola Herald*, published by Rick A. Fraser, and later J.W. Ellis.

As its original name implies, it served the area known as Nicola, a rich farming valley and lumbering district. The population was quite small until after the discovery of coal some seven miles from Nicola, which had an immediate impact on that community.

A general move was made to the new City of Merritt in 1908 when the paper's name was changed to the *Merritt Herald*. Early associates

Kamloops Blazers player AJ Baines. Photo by Brendan Halper, Kamloops This Week.

of the paper were Louis Lobsinger, who later retired to Kamloops, and Jim Ellis in Victoria.

In the early 1930s, Ernest B. Mayon assumed control of the newspaper and upon his death Mrs. Mayon carried on until 1960 when it was sold to Oswald Elsaesser.

Ernie Mayon was a president of the B.C. Weekly Newspapers Association in 1935-36. Mrs. Mayon was a well-known figure at association gatherings.

Elsaesser, meanwhile, was a journeyman printer but quickly became familiar with the newspaper end of the business. He owned the *Herald* for 30 years.

When Elsaesser took over the *Herald*, there were only four employees. After upgrading equipment and expanding the building, the total number of employees grew to 19. It was at this time he sold several shares to long-time employees Don Turner and Tami Geill to help him with the business. At that time the *Herald* operated its own letterpress and offset equipment and boasted one of the Interior's largest office supply stores.

In 1989, Mr. Elsaesser sold the entire operation due to a diabetic condition. He sold it to a partnership group of five people from Vancouver with Eric Cardwell and Bob Lambie of VanPress Printing being the principal owners. Cardwell and Lambie turned the operation of the business over to a group of five employees for one year, then appointed Tereza McDermid as publisher.

In 1993, Cardwell and Lambie sold the *Merritt Herald* to the Cariboo Press chain, while maintaining the print shop themselves, splitting the business in two within the same building. Some employees remained with the former owners and named themselves Merritt Printing, which still operates next door to the *Herald*.

Tereza McDermid remained as publisher, along with several employees from the previous regime. The letterpress and offset equipment was moved and the *Merritt Herald* went to the Cariboo Press facilities in Vernon for printing.

A year later, McDermid was succeeded as publisher by Dale Stoppler, the current publisher.

In 1995, the *Herald* made newspaper history when it won three Canadian Community Newspapers Association national newspaper awards. Beating out dozens of newspapers across Canada entered in the broadsheet category with circulation under 3,499, the *Herald* took first place for Best All-Around Newspaper, Best Front Page and Best Editorial Page. The *Herald* also received a CCNA blue ribbon award for taking first place in each general excellence classification.

That same year, the *Herald* moved from a broadsheet format to tabloid.

Today, the *Merritt Herald* under Cariboo Press, has modernized the newspaper with six full-time employees and covers a wide area of the Nicola Valley, including Lower Nicola, Nicola, Douglas Lake, Quilchena, Aspen Grove, Coldwater, Mamette Lake, Logan Lake and Spences Bridge, besides the City of Merritt.

In recent years, forestry has replaced mining as the primary industry in Merritt, but the development of rich deposits of copper by Highland Valley continues to help make Merritt a hive of industry.

MERRITT NEWS

Susan Holmberg had a dream to fulfill and she did it. She founded the *Merritt News* as an independent publisher in 1992. Business flourished and Holmberg soon had offers coming in to buy her little independent.

She ended up selling the paper to Ann Griffiths and Tom Douglas, along with Lower Mainland Publishing, in 1994, and opened a business services office in Merritt.

As part of the *News* network of papers, 6,300 residents in Merritt, Lower Nicola, Logan Lake, Quilchena and Douglas Lake can read local as well as regional news. In 1998 Nancy Chappell became the publisher and editor of the *Merritt News*.

NAKUSP, ARROW LAKES NEWS

The name Nakusp is of native origin meaning a sheltered bay. The town of Nakusp was built upon the shores of this crescent-shaped bay and overlooks snow-capped mountains. It is also the home of the *Arrow Lakes News*.

The current *Arrow Lakes News* is a latecomer into the newspaper industry of the valley, making its appearance on June 28, 1922 under the pen of Frank S. Rouleau. Before then, when Nakusp was still a mining town, numerous other weekly publications started up in the area. Most were short-lived. There was the *Slocan Record*, the *Silver Standard* of Nakusp, the *Slocan Mining Review* of Sandon, the *Arrow* of Burton City, the *Arrow Lakes Advocate*, the *Leaser* of New Denver, the *Kootenaian* of Kaslo, the *Paystreak* of Sandon, the *Kaslo Claim*, the *Slocan Herald*, and the *Ledge*.

When Rouleau started the *Arrow Lakes News* he published it from Kaslo. The inside four pages were printed in Regina; the balance finished off in Kaslo. This gave bulk to the publication, which somehow convinced the reader that he or she was getting a better newspaper.

In 1923, A.B.S. Stanley took over the paper, moving it to Nakusp. His son A.B.S. Stanley Jr., who was secretary of the B.C. Weekly Newspaper Association and a national director for years, followed him. In 1970, his son Denis took over management of the newspaper.

By then, Nakusp and area was better known for forestry than mining, though many tourists were attracted to visit some of the old mine workings.

Denis and his family ran the paper until 1994, when he sold it to George Manning's Small Town Press. Denis and family are still in town, operating a printing and stationary shop. Denis is working as chair of the Nakusp and Area FRBC Economic

Scott Sakatch, Invermere Valley Ecbo.

Development Board. His wife Judy is chair of the Nakusp and Area Community Health Council. Son Patrick is a firefighter, and in charge of the local July 1 fireworks display.

The *Arrow Lakes News* is still a small operation, running an average of 24 pages a week, covering news from several surrounding hamlets and villages, including Burton, Arrow Park, Fauquier, Edgewood, Hills, New Denver, Silverton and Trout Lake.

Forestry is perhaps the biggest ongoing issue in the *News*. There are three major Tree Farm Licences in the area, but no major mills. There are at least a dozen small mills, many of which are getting into value-added producing. Some growing pains are expected as the economy moves on to other things, and some businesses have found it impossible to survive.

The community is drawing together and a real push is on to pursue more value-added forestry and tourism as a replacement for the primary extraction that has kept the area humming economically for generations.

All other issues seem to pale beside economic survival, but community news, local politics, health and education, crime, and all that also fill out the pages at the *News*.

NELSON, KOOTENAY WEEKLY EXPRESS

I owe my success to ignorance. If I had known how long and what it would take to publish a successful community newspaper, I might never have started. Thank goodness for bad bookkeeping!

Nelson is a postcard community in the West Kootenay region of southeastern B.C. I arrived here in 1988 with the idea of opening a theatre cafe. I had the building all picked out, even though it was zoned residential and not commercial. I had envisioned a dynamic, "musician friendly" eatery with a monthly newsletter to promote upcoming performers. When the city refused my rezoning application to open the cafe, I opted for just the newsletter. Thus, the seed of the *Express* was sown.

Our first incarnation was as the monthly *What's On* magazine — an overly-ambitious attempt to give every local performer and every concert/play/performance some "ink." After two hectic years of publishing *What's On*, it became apparent that it was a monthly prescription for losing money. The only way to make it financially viable was to transform ourselves into a weekly — and not as a magazine, but as a newspaper. My goals changed, along with the perception of what I wanted to accomplish. In short, I wanted to give my community an open forum for contact and communication.

When I broke the news to my staff that we were going to go weekly, they were uniformly horrified, convinced there wouldn't be enough hours in the week to produce quality articles, let alone sell the advertising necessary to make it feasible. But reality has a way of turning negative thoughts into positive energy, and it did not take long for the staff to realize that, yes, it could be done!

I applied for membership in the BCYCNA shortly after switching to a weekly format but was told I had to maintain that status for at least two years before becoming a member. There were other requirements, too, including having an editorial each week. At first, I disagreed with this stipulation because I did not want to be perceived as telling my community what to think. Again, reality changed that perception. As the *Express* evolved into a true community "voice," I realized that our editorials, guest commentaries and opinion pieces were fulfilling the role I had sought all along: to provide our readers with new insights and attitudes and an opportunity to discuss the issues that affect us all. They are free to agree or disagree, of course, but we have made it our policy to consistently present both sides of whatever issues we choose to tackle.

Today, after 10 years as sole owner of the *Express*, I can only look ahead. I am never satisfied with resting on our laurels, because I firmly believe there is always a better way to do things. We have grown to become an integral part of the Nelson community — to the point where I am often stopped on the street by readers who simply want to tell me how important our newspaper is to their lives. That is a great feeling.

The *Express* has seen a decade of growth, wonder and (occasionally) trepidation — but our readers and advertisers have borne out what I only half believed when we started as a monthly in 1988: the weekly newspaper is a vital component in the life of every community. We will continue to humbly carry that responsibility into the new millennium.

—*Nelson Becker*

OLIVER CHRONICLE

The *Oliver Chronicle* is proud of its independent status — status it has held since the first publication date of the *Oliver Echo* on August 25, 1937.

At that time brothers H. Berryman (managing editor) and Dave Berryman (superintendent) operated the paper. They were the sons of Mr. and Mrs. Thomas Berryman, who also played active roles in running the family business. Until 1948 all type was set by hand and the *Echo* usually ran to four to six pages.

A lot has happened since that decade of hand setting. The name of the paper was changed to the *Oliver Chronicle* and *Osoyoos Observer* in 1939 and was a six-column broadsheet. In 1954, the papers switched their format to tabloid. Two years later the *Osoyoos Observer* was dropped and the paper became known simply as the *Chronicle*. Editor H. Berryman passed away in 1955. His brother and their parents took over the paper until 1950 when the *Chronicle* was sold to Don Somerville, circulation manager with the *Vancouver Sun*. Somerville was quick to change the *Chronicle* back to an over-sized broadsheet, the format it has retained to this day.

Somerville played a very active role in the B.C. Weekly Newspaper Association during his time as publisher of the *Chronicle*, serving as president in 1966. Before his retirement in 1986, Somerville spent a number of years representing B.C. as a director of the Canadian Weekly Newspapers Association.

Somerville sold the *Oliver Chronicle* in 1986 to Michael Newman, an Oliver orchardist who was looking for a change as well as a challenge. Newman apprenticed under Somerville for about six months before sealing the deal on the purchase of the *Chronicle*.

Newman brought fresh ideas to the *Chronicle* and also led the paper into the electronic age. Indeed, the *Oliver Chronicle* prides itself on being a progressive little paper. It was Newman who introduced the *Chronicle* to the computer age, taking his staff over all the bumps and curves in the road to becoming computer-literate.

The *Chronicle* has always embraced change that comes with improved technology. In June 1995, it became the first weekly newspaper in Canada to establish a presence on the Internet. Its home page, found at *oliver-chronicle.com*, boasts global readership, often receiving letters to the editor from as far afield as Europe, Australia and Asia. Readers, wherever they may find themselves, have quick access to front-page stories, editorials and classified ads. The web page is updated just as each issue of the *Chronicle* goes to press. In fact, many readers have picked up the habit of checking out *oliver-chronicle.com* before the hard copy hits the streets!

The *Chronicle's* latest step toward the millennium has been the use of digital photography, which allows colour pictures to be easily reproduced. The new technology was tested in the November 12, 1997 issue; since then the *Chronicle* has become a brighter read.

OSOYOOS TIMES

Cooperation has always played an important part in the development of Osoyoos and was instrumental in the establishment of the *Osoyoos Times* in 1947.

A young couple who literally drifted into the area in search of a place where they could settle and make a living founded the paper. The Chamber of Commerce was looking for someone to start a local paper. Stan and Rosemary Stodola jumped at the chance. And after arranging with the *Penticton Herald* to be the printers, a typewriter was purchased, a few advertisement spaces were sold to local merchants, and soon enough the *Osoyoos Times*, all 10 pages of it, was rolling of the presses for the 1,200 local residents.

Two years after that the *Times* put in a hand-fed platen press for some job printing and two years after that an entire plant was established.

"It took cooperation to keep the paper going when I took sick for four months in 1952," says Stan Stodola. "Rosemary, with help from the late Jack Murray of the *Penticton Herald*, plus wonderful cooperation of the community, saw the paper through that difficult time."

New publisher Patrick Turner along with Chris Stodola continue that cooperation and the legacy the Stodolas created at the *Osoyoos Times*.

PEACHLAND SIGNAL

Howard and Felicity Fuchs took a little bit of capital and a whole bunch of energy to start the *Peachland Signal* in 1991. The 12-page newspaper was a homespun publication that carved a niche for itself in Peachland.

After five years, and many long hours, they sold the paper to Jim Clark, who left his duties as publisher of the *Kelowna Capital News* to own and operate his own paper.

Because it's a bedroom community to larger towns in the area, Peachland, by itself, does not offer the kind of advertising revenue a paper needs to survive and grow in the long term. As a result, one of Clark's first acts as owner was to change the *Peachland Signal* from a free paper to paid subscriptions. Another was to actively solicit advertising from the surrounding larger centres. These moves helped Clark expand and redesign the paper as well as assure the publication a long and prosperous future.

PENTICTON WESTERN NEWS ADVERTISER

 It began modestly more than 30 years ago when a group of teachers created a vehicle for advertising.

Soon the *Western Advertiser* became a household name for people interested in buying and selling.

However, in the past few years the *Penticton Western News Advertiser* has accelerated into a twice-weekly newspaper with a strong emphasis on news coverage of Penticton and the South Okanagan.

In the fall of 1997, the *Western* was accepted as a member of the BCYCNA.

Penticton Western *publisher, Juanita Gibney, 1998.*

"I felt it was time the *Western* became a member of the provincial community newspaper organization," says publisher Juanita Gibney. "I feel there is great benefit and am pleased to participate in the CCNA verified circulation auditing program. It's good for us and good for our readers."

Among the founding teachers 30 years before was Bill Barlee, well-known B.C. historian and a former New Democrat cabinet minister. Louise Hunt took over ownership during the 1960s and eventually sold the *Western* to a local couple, Fred and Veronica Miner.

Its first office, on Westminster Avenue in downtown Penticton, "was really just a hole in the wall," says Simon Groot, a retired advertising sales person.

Cathy Proteau, a *Western* advertising sales representative for 19 years, chuckles about the office and the changes she has seen.

"We had cardboard walls and shared a telephone," she says standing in a new two-storey office building in Penticton's Industrial Park. "Now I have a workstation and my own phone — that's a big difference."

In 1983, Pat Duncan become publisher and the *Western* moved into a former car dealership building on the southern shore of Okanagan Lake. The Front Street office served the growing operation for 13 years.

During the 1980s, the *Western Advertiser* was purchased by Bowes Publishers Limited after company founder Jim Bowes saw it during a visit to the Okanagan.

The paper became part of a national group of community newspapers under the ownership of Sun Media Corporation, which by 1998 consisted of more then 100 properties.

Over the years, the *Western Advertiser* underwent a series of technological changes.

"In 1983, the *Western's* typesetting capability consisted of a strip printer with three styles of type for headlines and a Remington typewriter to type in advertising copy," says former publisher Pat Duncan.

In 1984 it advanced to Compugraphic typesetters at a cost of cost $60,000 each.

"Today they are only good for boat anchors," he says. One of the units was donated to the Penticton Museum for a local technological collection.

In 1988, the *Western* switched its composing system to Apple Macintosh computers "which have 100 times the flexibility and creativity of the old Compugraphic at a fraction of the cost," says Duncan, now publisher of the *Summerland Review*.

The weekly jumped to twice a week (Tuesdays and Fridays), was redesigned and increased its editorial staff in 1995. It started to play a stronger news, as well as advertising, role in Penticton and the South Okanagan.

Western News staff became regulars at festivals and fires, at city council and school board meetings, at sports and cultural events, and at gatherings of business people, wine makers, politicians, orchardists and other local newsmakers. Stories stirred readers and editorials challenged the community.

In 1996, the *Western* made its most recent move to Penticton's Industrial Park. The news, advertising and circulation staff took over a new addition to the Webco West building on Camrose Street.

Webco West, also owned by Bowes Publishers Limited, is a web press plant. It prints the Western, its sister newspaper the *Summerland Review* and more than a dozen independent community newspapers serving southern British Columbia and northern Washington State as well as flyers, magazines and books.

Technological improvements such as pagination and increased colour capacity gave it more flexibility to serve its advertisers and readers.

In 1997, Juanita Gibney, a Bowes Publishers employee since 1979, moved from her position as publisher of the *Summerland Review* to become publisher of the *Western News Advertiser*.

—Wayne Campbell

PRINCETON, SIMILKAMEEN SPOTLIGHT

The *Similkameen Spotlight* celebrated 50 years of continuous publishing in 1998 — but the Princeton-based newspaper's headquarters are perhaps as interesting as the people and events it has covered over the years.

The town's first newspaper was called the *Star*. It hit the streets some time after the turn of the century and was published out of a former house of ill repute. According to one of Princeton's history books (published by the *Spotlight* in 1979), the first newspaper was produced out of a whorehouse run by a "Negro" lady. The first editor was E. Anderson, who was succeeded by J. Wright, Joe Brown, Dave Taylor and eventually Dr. J.C. Goodfellow.

The *Star* discontinued publishing in 1945, before resurfacing as the *Valley Spotlight* under the ownership of A. Gaustin. Gaustin sold the *Spotlight* in 1948 to Cam Hooper who ran the newspaper until

1955 when it again changed hands and became the property of Laurie Currie. Affectionately known as "Scoop," Currie went on to become the longest serving publisher/editor in the *Spotlight's* history. Currie recalled walking into the office of then owner Hooper and asking if the newspaper was for sale.

"Hooper was very unhappy at the time and says, 'Sure, you can have it for 10 cents.'"

Although they didn't have much money at the time, Currie and his wife, Sonja, managed to scrape up the down payment. "It wasn't for 10 cents, but I did buy a newspaper and, of course, I didn't have a clue . . ."

It was a rocky start for the fledgling owner as the Linotype operator, "a kid trained in prison," gave his notice just two weeks into Currie's tenure. Fortunately, Currie's mechanical background allowed him to take over and keep the *Spotlight* from missing a deadline.

A sponsored Hungarian refugee helped bring out the best in the *Spotlight*, recalled Currie, as the innovative European used a "rubber diaper to bring up the image on the press.

"He put this diaper behind the big plate and it sure as hell worked."

Perhaps Currie's most infamous moment came the day he had to fire his mother-in-law.

"It got to the point where that bloody Linotype was completely haywire and she was over her head mechanically," he says. "She was so determined at the time we were helping each other, but it got to where I just couldn't cope with it anymore.

"t was really tough too, and it certainly bothered me a long time . . . but we got over it."

Currie tried to keep up with modern technological changes as they occurred in the industry and was a pioneer in several aspects.

"We were the first bonafide newspaper in the province of B.C. to change over from cold type to offset."

Despite the unrelenting pressures of deadlines, mothers-in-law and customers, Currie always managed to keep his sense of humour. The *Spotlight* also used an historic granite slab, once used in a local morgue.

One of Currie's favourite jokes was to dab red ink on the slab and tell visitors it was the bloody remains of past stiffs on the block.

"It used to really tear them," he says.

Currie sold the *Spotlight*, after a 26-year career, to employee Fred

Heck and his family. The Hecks ran the *Spotlight* from 1981 until 1995 when they turned it over to Ed and Lynn Vermette. The *Spotlight* again changed hands in July 1997 when Small Town Press Ltd. purchased the venerable community newspaper.

REVELSTOKE TIMES REVIEW

The City of Revelstoke turned 100 in 1999. Named after the first Lord Revelstoke, whose British banking firm was responsible for saving Canada's National Dream from financial ruin, the town's history is linked with the building of the Canadian Pacific Railway and includes the Last Spike site at Craigellachie among its historic treasures.

For more than a century Revelstoke has had about half a dozen different homegrown newspapers providing residents with information about local events and happenings throughout the province, Canada and the world. For a few brief months during the late 1890s, the little railway town even boasted a four-page daily, *The Herald*, before circumstances pushed that paper under.

The *Times Review* is the latest incarnation of Revelstoke's newspaper tradition, resulting from the merger of two local independents, the old *Revelstoke Review* and the younger *Revelstoke Times*.

The *Review* was founded in 1914 by W.H. Bohannan who moved his plant from Chase to Revelstoke intending to create a Liberal newspaper to "smash the McBride-Bowser machine" as the paper's first slogan stated. The *Review* at the time carried on the tradition of many early newspapers of close identification with a particular political party. Its rival, the *Mail-Herald*, was a staunch Tory paper. Arvid Lundell, one of the carriers for the early *Review*, later became the newspaper's publisher. The *Review* eventually became a Lundell family possession.

The *Mail-Herald* folded, leaving the *Review* the sole newspaper in Revelstoke, barring one or two short-lived rivals, for more than seven decades until 1985 when two friends, Penny Graham and Sue Oliver, decided to start *The Front Row Centre*.

The monthly publication focused at first on "soft news," community events and entertainment with Graham and Oliver doing everything from gathering information, taking pictures, laying out and pasting up the pages, driving the flats to the printer and then delivering the finished product to doorsteps all over town. The two were early pioneers of the desktop publishing revolution, using a Macintosh system for design and editorial work.

From a monthly, *The Front Row Centre* started coming out every fortnight, then weekly. It also began covering more hard news and sports as well as changing its name to *The Revelstoke Times*.

The beginning of the 90s saw Revelstoke's two papers become part of the WestMount Group based in Banff. The Lundell family sold out their interest in the *Review* while Graham and Oliver exchanged their interest in the *Times* for shares in WestMount. The two papers were merged into one, the *Times Review*, which came out twice a week for a while but reverted back to weekly status as ad support revenue dropped with the tightening local economy.

In 1998, the Bowes Publishers Ltd., part of the Sun syndicate, bought WestMount. Becoming part of the Sun chain of daily and community newspapers has had little, if any, effect on the *Times Review's* goal of trying to provide readers with the news they need to know, the news they'd like to know and the news they might be interested to know.

—*Gregg Chamberlain*

Salmon Arm Observer/ Sicamous Eagle Valley News/ Shuswap Market News

Salmon Arm, "Gem of the Shuswap," is a tourism Mecca, where agriculture, forestry and the "retirement industry" also flourish. Situated on the shores of Shuswap Lake and on the Trans-Canada Highway, it is midway between Vancouver and Calgary.

The *Salmon Arm Observer* has been the paper of record in the community for more than 90 years and in that time has captured an impressive array of honours and awards.

The paper was founded October 7, 1907, by the brothers William and Henry Fraser, who had previously operated a small paper in nearby Enderby. As was almost always the case, job printing and,

Gord Priestman, editor of the Salmon Arm Observer *for over 30 years, 1998.*

later stationery sales, became integral parts of the business.

A little over two years after opening, the Frasers sold to George W. Armstrong, an old-time newsman from Vernon, who ran things for six years before deciding to trade his pen for a plough. William Fraser and another brother, Ron, resumed control again briefly before selling to Horace E. Moore in 1915.

Six years later 21-year *Kamloops Standard-Sentinel* veteran W.W. Bishop took the helm, with Keith Wiles as his editor. Seven years later the *Observer* changed hands yet again, with Irish-born Peter Campbell coming from the *Cowichan Leader* as publisher/editor. His son, Donald, became production foreman. Don took a keen interest in the B.C. Weekly Newspapers Association, serving long on the executive and being elected president in 1942.

After 16 years the Campbells sold the paper to Frank Marshall and family. Frank, who had been editor of the *New Westminster Columbian*, used his extensive background to create a flourishing paper to serve the entire Shuswap community. He also took on a prominent role with the weekly newspapers association.

Four years after arriving, Frank and Laura Marshall constructed the present *Observer* building, which opened in 1948.

Progress continued with modernization, technological upgrades and a record of awards. All those traditions continued after Frank's death in 1964 when son Dennis took the helm. Dennis enjoyed the services of well-known newsman Rollie Rose as editor for a year or so in the mid-60s. Present editor Gordon Priestman succeeded Rose in 1967. Several expansions later, in February 1973, Dennis Marshall shepherded the change to offset printing with the help of longtime shop foreman Floyd Carey, current foreman Graham Redman, who has been with the *Observer* 44 years, and Gene Luduc, a production staff member since 1960.

The Marshall era ended, after 32 years, when Dennis split off the stationery business, which was now in a separate building. The paper and printing end was sold in 1976 to former *Vernon News* owner Frank Harris. The latter's daughter, Lynne, and her husband, Ian Wickett, became partners and the latter took over as manager.

Under Wickett, who was active in the BCYCNA, technological improvements continued, including conversion from typewriters to the computer age, but the emphasis remained on community service and quality. However, the phasing out of independents was well under way by the 80s and thus it was that, in September of 1987, the Harris-Wickett interests were sold to David Black's Cariboo Press and became part of a growing chain.

Ian Wickett remained as publisher for about a year, during which time the job printing operation was sold to two former *Observer* production staff members, Bernie and Gary Hucul, who continue to operate it as of this writing.

Wickett was succeeded as publisher by Robin Campbell for about three years, by Brian Smart for a year, then by Curt Duddy who had the reins for three years before leaving to open the *Prince George Free Press* for Cariboo Press.

In June of 1995, longtime Salmon Arm resident Ron Lovestone succeeded Duddy.

The staff now numbers more than 25, plus hundreds of part-timers, correspondents and carriers. The paid-circulation *Observer*, which focuses on Salmon Arm, has been joined by the free-distribution *Shuswap Market News*, which covers the entire Shuswap area, the *Eagle Valley News* in Sicamous and a number of special publication such as a real estate guide and tourism directory.

But publication changes and staff changes aside, the aim of everyone connected with the blue ribbon-winning *Observer* remains exactly as stated by the Fraser brothers way back in 1907: to give the community as good a newspaper as possible — then work a little harder to make it even better.

SALMON ARM/ SHUSWAP SUN

 "A real experience" is how publisher Robin Campbell describes his foray into newspaper ownership and administration.

Campbell, who had worked his way through the newspaper business first in advertising at the *Kamloops Daily News* and then as publisher at the *Salmon Arm Observer*, was only somewhat prepared for the day-to-day pressures surrounding ownership.

"When I purchased the *Sun* from original owners Bruce and Jean Butterfield in 1991, I really had no idea what I was getting into," he says. "It was the ultimate learning curve."

The *Sun* began publication in 1983 in nearby Sorento. Produced from their home, the Butterfields had high hopes for a paper, which was located in one of B.C.'s most competitive markets.

By 1989, the paper had moved to Salmon Arm, via a stop in Chase for a couple of years, and now had a real office and real employees and had begun to attract some takeover bids. When Campbell came along and purchased the *Sun*, the Butterfields let go of their baby, proud of what they had achieved.

"They handed us a fine publication with a great staff," says Campbell. "It was a great way to start and easy to build on."

The *Sun* was already on the fast track to success when Lower Mainland Publishing bought the paper in 1994.

"Lower Mainland Publishing is such a great company to be part of," says Campbell. "When they offered to purchase the paper, they also gave us complete autonomy. That was very important to me."

Having Lower Mainland Publishing in charge of the dollars and cents took a huge weight off Campbell's shoulders. Now he could concentrate on making sure the product was top notch.

"Thanks to an amazing staff here at the *Sun*, I can proudly boast that we are producing a credible community paper," says Campbell. "And if it wasn't credible, believe me, the residents in this area would let us know."

The *Salmon Arm/Shuswap Sun's* future looks bright indeed. And for Robin Campbell, things could not be any better.

"I run a great paper and I live in a little piece of paradise. Need I say more?"

SPARWOOD, THE ELK VALLEY MINER

A hundred years ago, coal began to be mined in the valley of the Elk River in southeastern British Columbia. It was during that time, on September 9, 1898, a gentleman formerly with the *Vernon News* arrived.

His name was George G. Henderson, and he was setting up shop as publisher, reporter, advertising manager for the *Fernie Free Press*. Soon enough, Henderson would have competition, the peripatetic publisher from the West Kootenay and Boundary country, Col. R.T. Lowery, who started the *Ledger*.

Lowery's Fernie paper would end up, like so many papers, as a tombstone — unable to compete with Henderson's *Free Press*. At this point, it might be right and proper to pay tribute to a few other tombstones of journalism in the valley: The *Ledger, District Ledger, The Morrissey Miner, Hosmer News, Michel Reporter, Sparwood-Elkford News, Crowsnest Clarion* and *Fernie Optimist*.

On April 1, 1984 — April Fool's Day — a new paper, without warning, appeared in Sparwood to compete with the *Free Press*. It was called *The Elk Valley Miner*.

It is rumoured that the publisher of the *Free Press*, on hearing the news, banged his fist on his desk and with the other hand pointed toward Sparwood and cried out: "We'll bury you!"

That publisher is long gone and *The Elk Valley Miner* survives as a formidable rival to the *Free Press*. The original publisher of the *Elk Valley Miner* was Ted Moser, a former senior editor of the Toronto *Globe & Mail*, who returned to his home town of Blairmore to run the already established weekly, *The Promoter*.

Moser, a seasoned journalist but not a seasoned businessmen, hired a Sparwood accountant by the name of Fritz Brockel. They were a good team, and for a while it looked as if the *Free Press* would become yet another newspaper tombstone. But the *Free Press* prevailed after media mogul Conrad Black entered the scene by adding the newspaper to his stable.

Over coffee on a warm day in August 1993, Moser told Brockel he was going to retire and a deal was entered into whereby Brockel the accountant would buy out Moser the journalist.

In 1994, *The Elk Valley Miner* entered the computer age: new sophisticated equipment was in place and a highly skilled staff, both in the back shop and the editorial room, had been hired.

In addition, to give the *Free Press* a run for its money, the Miner opened an editorial and sales offices in Fernie. And until January 1997, the paper was sent to Taber, Alberta, for printing. But when Brockel made a trip down to Kalispell, Montana, to visit the *Inter-Lake News*, which had just installed a new press that offered full colour printing, it was a case of love at first sight and a printing agreement was soon entered into. The deal helped the paper's bottom line and kept things competitive. Today, staff at *The Elk Valley Miner* are proud to run the only independent weekly newspaper in the East Kootenay region.

—Bruce Ramsey

OKANAGAN FALLS, SOUTH OKANAGAN REVIEW

The first newspaper in Okanagan Falls was the *Okanagan Mining Review*, which published six issues from August to November in 1893. The editor was Dr. R. Mathisone, a dentist who was part of the W.J. Snodgrass syndicate hoping to develop Okanagan Falls into the economic centre of the province. The paper promoted Okanagan Falls as the geographic, industrial, agricultural, mining, manufacturing and railway centre of the southern interior of the province. It neglected to mention the nearest railway was at the north end of Okanagan Lake, west of Vernon, over 130 kilometres away.

There were several attempts to revive the paper over the years without much success. In the late 1970s Charles and Margaret Hayes emigrated to Canada from Kenya, where he founded the East Africa Press Exchange, a multi-media organization serving the world with news and photos about Kenya. He also started the weekly newspaper, the *Nation*, and later founded the magazine *Africana*, which became an internationally known conservation magazine. Hayes and his publications were awarded the Franklin Mint medals for services to wildlife conservation.

Upon arriving in Canada Margaret and Charles settled in Okanagan Falls where the publishing bug soon got to them again. To fill the void left when the *Okanagan Falls Viewpoint* ceased publication, Hayes created the name *Review*. The *South Okanagan Review* has been serving the area ever since.

When Hayes decided to retire he sold the paper to Dave Obee, a newspaperman from Calgary, in 1995. Two years later Obee sold the *Review* to Greg Masson, who ran it for a brief period before selling to veteran newspaperman Ron Loftus. Loftus was the founder of the *Royal City Record* in New Westminster and had worked at the *Vancouver Sun* for 35 years. Since taking over the *Review* in September of 1997, the paper has expanded its circulation from 1,200 to 5,500 and now serves Okanagan Falls, Oliver and Keremeos and all points in between. In June the *Review* started publishing the *Lifestyles Review*, a monthly publication distributing 12,000 papers from Penticton to Osoyoos.

—Greg Masson

SUMMERLAND REVIEW

 The *Summerland Review*, founded in 1908 by J.F. Watkins, has seen a number of changes over the years.

A.T. Robinson, one of three brothers who developed Summerland, Peachland and Naramata, was the next publisher.

He was followed by Tom Collinge but he soon sold to Ralph E. White, who was editor and publisher until he sold the paper to take over the *Kamloops Sentinel* in 1925.

Walter M. Wright — known as Seldom Wright — was editor for a short time until the Penticton Herald Printing & Publishing Co. Limited, with R.J. McDougall as controller, acquired the paper.

By the late 1920s, the *Review* had become just a couple of pages in the *Penticton Herald* and in 1928 it ceased entirely.

In 1946, J.R. (Tim) Armstrong and George Fudge, who had previously served in the Canadian Army, bought some printing equipment which had been stored in Abbotsford and re-established the *Review*. Their first edition came out June 6, one month after they had left the army. Armstrong later bought out Fudge's interest and was joined by Tom McKay.

In 1953, Gordon Crockett bought the paper and operated it for three years before selling to Syd Godber, who was publisher until 1958. Eric Williams took over until 1965, when Keith Berg assumed ownership. Under Berg, printing of the paper was moved from Summerland to Oliver. He also took over the *Summerland Bulletin* and discontinued its publication. He resigned as editor of the *Review* in 1971.

Dave Gamble bought the paper and took over the duties of editor-publisher from 1971 to 1989, when the paper was sold to Bowes Publishers.

Ron Moropito was publisher until 1993 when Juanita Gibney took over. Pat Duncan became publisher of the *Review* in March 1997.

The *Review* became a colourful, reformatted tabloid in late 1996 and continues to be a strong voice in a highly controversial city of 11,500 spirited people.

Summerland adopted an Olde English theme in the early 1990s and all new commercial downtown buildings have adopted the Olde English facade.

Nestled on the west side of Okanagan Lake, Summerland has become known for its many festivals during the year, including the Children's Festival in April, Action Festival in June, Taste of Summerland in August and Festival of Lights in November.

All the festivals draw thousands of people from the Okanagan and beyond and the *Review* is there for it all.

VERNON SUN

 June 2, 1996 dawned bright and sunny and there was something new for North Okanagan residents to look forward to.

The *Vernon Sun* became a bold and bright addition to the local scene, offering readers an enterprising and entertaining addition to existing newspapers in the area.

Founding publisher Wayne Porter, who conceived the newspaper with Gary Johnston, says that from the start the goal was to create a product that took a fair and balanced approach to news but didn't shy away from the tough and controversial stories.

"Our job, first and foremost, is to inform our readers and sometimes you have to step on a few toes to do that," says Porter.

Readers immediately embraced the newsy format and Porter was thrilled by the paper's early success. But continuous hard work is what keeps readers.

The editorial and advertising departments have won several awards and there is a continuous program to improve all aspects of the paper.

Rob DeMone was the *Sun's* first managing editor and set the course for the look of the paper. DeMone moved on to a sister paper, *Chilliwack Times*, in the fall of 1997 and Dean Broughton took over the helm.

The *Sun's* senior reporter, Russ Niles, has been decorated for his insightful wit, winning second place in the Suburban Newspapers of America's editorial competition for best column writing.

Sun photographer Desmond Murray was also recognized for his photographic prowess, winning second in the SNA's photo competition.

From the beginning, the *Sun* has been associated with Lower Mainland Publishing Ltd., giving it access to some of the best technical support people in the business as well as participation in successful group advertising programs that gives clients exposure in six newspapers throughout the region. The *Sun* also became the first paper in the area to offer Internet classified advertising.

There is intense competition in the local market and the *Sun* is constantly looking for ways to serve customers better and more efficiently.

"There's no doubt that we're in a challenging situation but our readers and advertisers are encouraging us to stick to our original concept and deliver them an informative and entertaining package every Thursday and Sunday," Porter says.

Distribution is an important aspect of the *Sun*. More than 29,000 papers are delivered each publication day and the paper prides itself in the individual attention it gives many rural customers. A large percentage of rural customers have individual tubes at the foot of their driveways instead of a drop box by their group mailbox.

The *Sun* has about 15 full-time employees and about 200 part-time carriers and drivers.

VERNON, THE MORNING STAR

 The Morning Star started as an independent community newspaper in June 1988.

The four co-founders, Bill Allum, Don Kendall, Ken McCluskey and Wayne Porter, had all previously worked for the *Vernon Daily News*. Several other staff members left the *Daily News* to join the quartet of entrepreneurs at the new paper.

Their vision was to create a newspaper that would become an important part of their community. But seven months of unprecedented growth created cash flow problems for the partners. A potential financial crisis, combined with the rumours that the independent publisher who printed their newspaper in Vernon might be closing, prompted the owners to sell to Cariboo Press in December 1988. The following year, the newspaper went from twice a week to three times a week and in 1990 one of the competitors in the North Okanagan, the *Vernon News Advertiser*, ceased publication.

In the early-90s, McCluskey and later Porter left the newspaper to pursue careers in real estate. Allum, who had named the paper (the combination of *Morning* for morning delivery and *Star* in recognition of the Silver Star ski area), was the general manager until he died of cancer in 1994.

Kendall remained as the publisher and a shareholder through *The Morning Star's* first decade. He joined the board of directors of the B.C. and Yukon Community Newspapers Association in 1994 and became the group's first vice-president in 1997.

Glen Mitchell, who was the first reporter hired by Kendall in '88, left in 1990 to become editor of the *Salmon Arm Observer*. Two years later, he returned to *The Morning Star* as managing editor.

The Vernon Daily News, owned by Thomson Newspapers, ceased publication in 1996. It was a sad end for a newspaper that had won numerous awards, as an independent biweekly, prior to being purchased by Thomson and turned into a small town daily in the early-1970s.

In *The Morning Star's* first decade, the circulation grew from 24,000 to 30,200 as the North Okanagan attracted new residents from across the country. The staff at the newspaper also grew, from 12 to 46 full-time employees. Cariboo Press opened a regional press

Publisher Don Kendall, left, and General Manager Bill Allum take time out from their regular duties to insert flyers during the early days of The (Vernon) Morning Star. *Kendall and Allum were two of the four founders of the newspaper.* The Mornng Star *became part of the Cariboo Press chain in December, 1988.*

and mailroom division in Vernon in 1990, which employs an additional 50-60 full and part-time workers.

From its inception, the management and staff have taken pride in their newspaper and their position in the community. Twice *The Morning Star* has won the Greater Vernon Chamber of Commerce's Community Booster Award. In 1992, the newspaper earned the Yellow Pages Small Business Award. That same year, Kendall was named the North Okanagan Community Life Society's Good Guy of the Year.

The Morning Star won more than 40 provincial and national newspaper association awards in its first decade, in the highest circulation categories, where most papers are from suburban centres. Perhaps the most prestigious award, and the one that the staff is most proud of, is the Hoodspith Award, presented by the CCNA for outstanding community service. *The Morning Star* was presented with the award in 1992 and five years later became the first newspaper to win the award for a second time.

When asked the reason for his newspaper's success Kendall says, without hesitation, "Great people."

WINFIELD, THE LAKE COUNTRY CALENDAR

The Winfield Calendar became a weekly tabloid community newspaper in September of 1979. Two local residents, Jack McCarthy and John Gable, made the move to operate a weekly, serving the three communities of Winfield, Oyama and Okanagan Centre, following the purchase of the *Winfield Calendar*, a community newsletter that was published monthly by the Winfield Ladies Hospital Auxiliary.

The Winfield Women's Institute introduced the original newsletter to the community in February of 1951 as *The Calendar*. The monthly publication, which was run off on a Gestetner duplicator, listed births, deaths, community events, notices of baby clinics, progress reports on the finishing of the community hall and a list of new families that had moved into the district. The three communities that were served were primarily agricultural in nature with a population of less than 800 people in 1951.

That first newsletter consisted of a single sheet of paper printed on one side.

By 1979, the population of Winfield had grown to 3,500 people and the monthly edition of *The Calendar* was 36-40 printed pages — on both sides. A full-page ad sold for $25, a half page for $15 and a quarter page for $10. Birth and death announcements were placed free of charge. The publication was delivered through the mail free of charge to every household in Winfield.

Following their purchase of *The Calendar*, Gable and McCarthy began to sell subscriptions to their weekly publication. After their initial subscription drive they were publishing approximately 2,000 copies a week which were distributed through Canada Post and over the counter in local stores.

Just nine months after the weekly publication was launched John Gable died of cancer and Jack McCarthy took on the task of running the publication himself. He became the publisher-editor, reporter, salesperson, and along with his wife Marion, nursed the weekly newspaper through those early years. McCarthy is still in charge of the day-to-day operations as the publisher-owner of *The Calendar*.

The Calendar changed its masthead to the *Lake Country Calendar* in May of 1995, when B.C.'s newest municipality, Lake Country, was incorporated. Lake Country is made up of the four communities of Winfield, Oyama, Okanagan Centre and Carrs Landing.

On staff at *The Calendar* is longtime typographer and production manager, Debbie Haber, who began working for the paper in October of 1979. She and publisher McCarthy mark their 20th year with the newspaper in 1999.

Among the contributing writers are Bryan Cooney, 90, whose weekly column, *Thin Ink*, has appeared every week since late 1979. Cooney began writing *Thin Ink* back in the late 40s.

Gardening columnist Alice Makowichuk joined *The Calendar* as a regular weekly columnist in 1981 and contributed until January of 1998. Her column still appears monthly and in special issues of *The Calendar*. *The Calendar's* current editor, Bud Mortenson, wrote his first guest editorial in *The Calendar* when he was only 16 years old and a student at Winfield's George Elliot Secondary School. Mortenson joined *The Calendar* as a reporter-computer whiz when the publication first embraced desktop publishing back in 1986. After college and a sojourn in the mining industry, Mortenson returned to *The Calendar* in 1990 and became editor in 1992.

Photographer Steve Kidd joined *The Calendar* in 1995, following the retirement of long-time *Calendar* photographer Bill Haden.

—*Deb Haber*

CENTRAL INTERIOR / THE NORTH

QUESNEL • CARIBOO

OBSERVER

SINCE 1908

Volume 13, Issue 24   93¢   Wednesday, June 17,1998
plus GST

The Valley

Sentinel

TERRACE

STANDARD

Yukon News

Northern
Sentinel

100 MILE HOUSE FREE PRESS

The *100 Mile House Free Press* serves the vibrant South Cariboo community of nearly 20,000 people over the wide-open spaces of the Interior plateau.

The award-winning tabloid weekly is part of the Cariboo Press group of newspapers, yet it is firmly rooted in its home town. Although the name of 100 Mile House dates back to the Cariboo Gold Rush of the 1860s, the town did not come into being until after the Second World War.

A stopping house on the old Gold Rush trail, the original 100 Mile House burned down in 1930, replaced by the 100 Mile Lodge, built by pioneer landowner Lord Martin Cecil. His father, the Marquess of Exeter, had purchased the ranch area in 1912.

Photo by Jay Bullock, 100 Mile Free Press.

A pair of small papers served the tiny ranching and lumber community, the *South Cariboo News Advertiser*, started in 1955, and the *Hundred Mile Herald*, founded in 1960.

The *Herald* was published by Clive Stangoe of Cariboo Press in Williams Lake, an hour to the north. The founding editor was Carol Shaw, a former *Vancouver Sun* reporter. The small operation followed the community's growth to incorporation in 1965.

At the same time, Stangoe's Cariboo Press was busy fending off some fierce competition in Williams Lake, prompting the sale of the *Herald*.

Both South Cariboo publications were purchased by Herald House Publishing, a 100 Mile-based subsidiary of the Emissaries of Divine Light, a religious sect headed by Lord Martin Cecil that was very prominent in the community at that time. The new broadsheet publication was under the banner *100 Mile House News-Herald*, with J.E. (Joe) Maynard as publisher and Carol Shaw continuing as editor for a time.

Within a couple of years, with Chris Foster as editor, the *News-Herald* was named the *Free Press*.

Early production was costly and time-consuming, with writing and ad layout being done in 100 Mile, paste-up being done at Cariboo Press in Williams Lake, followed by printing in Quesnel. Herald House ran into financial difficulties and by 1967 was on the verge of bankruptcy.

Fresh capital and business acumen arrived with J.F. Traff, a former editor and advertising manager with two Powell River publications.

The paper grew in size and quality. By 1969, it was winning Canadian Weekly Newspaper Association awards for community service, general excellence, news, outdoor, feature writing and photography — a tradition that continues today.

The *Free Press* has been awarded many national and provincial awards for the paper, its special features and its writers and photographers, and won the B.C. Press Foundation award for Best News for its 1995 coverage of the nearby Gustafsen Lake standoff.

Editors have included David Ish, John Simituk, Gordon Kellett, David Stubbs, Paul Luft, Curtis Pollock and Steven Frasher.

Fred Traff was publisher until 1984, followed by Luke Vorstermans (1984-90) and Kevin Marks (1990-93). In November 1992,

Photo by Jim Sinclair, 100 Mile House Free Press.

Cariboo Press purchased the paper from Herald House. Publishers since then have been Terry Gibbons (1993-97), Lorne Doerkson (1997-98) and Chris Nickless.

The *Free Press* office employs 15 regular staff members in all departments. In addition to the publisher and editor, there are three advertising representatives, two reporters, a photo-darkroom specialist, two compositors, three production assistants and two front office staff. The in-house editorial content is bolstered by the contributions of six local columnists and 12 dependable correspondents covering outlying areas, including Clinton, Canim Lake, Forest Grove, Lone Butte, Bridge Lake, 108 Mile Ranch and Lac la Hache.

BURNS LAKE, LAKES DISTRICT NEWS/HOUSTON TODAY

Publisher Hank Hoornenborg combined the *Lakes District News* and *Houston Today* into one newspaper in 1974. In July of 1975, Bill and Jacqui Graham purchased the combined newspapers.

Bill had been a newspaper reporter and Jacqui a radio copywriter.

The couple moved the main office from Houston to Burns Lake and appointed Mary Ann Ruiter manager of the Houston end. The broadsheet newspaper was published in two or more sections with front pages for Houston and Burns Lake. The sections were stuffed

Tom MacDougall, Editor, Burns Lake District News, 1998.

Pat Turkki of the Burns Lake News *received an honorable mention prize from Doug Cooper of MacMillan Bloedel at an annual* BCYCNA *convention, circa late 1970s. The judges commented that they were charmed and entertained by the warmth and human perception, and the very good writing, that went into a series of columns about people and life in rural northern British Columbia.*

to show the appropriate front page in each community. In 1978, the *Babine Bulletin* of Granisle was acquired, and a third front page was added to the regional package.

Regional growth in the years between 1975 and 1980 caused the paper to swell from 12 pages per week to more than 24. The operation moved twice, finally locating in an extensively renovated heritage building, Burns Lake's former Provincial Police headquarters, built in 1923. The *Lakes District News/Houston Today* was one of the first small weeklies to adopt innovative computer technology, introducing in 1978 computer workstations and telephone data transfer between the two offices.

Under the Grahams, the newspapers emphasized aggressive coverage of local news, well-displayed photographs and colourful local columnists. Columnists Pat Turkki and Bob Harkins won MacMillan Bloedel awards for their writing.

The Grahams sold their newspaper operation to Cariboo Press in 1980, and the Houston and Burns Lake papers were subsequently split apart and continue as such to this day.

JACK THE GHOST

It was late at night when I first smelled the cigar.

I always worked late at the paper on Fridays and although I had heard rumours of a ghost at *LD News*, I was skeptical. Our staff had often told me about unexplained things that happened and told me it was Jack, the ghost. They seemed very blase about it, though.

"Don't worry, Jack hasn't hurt anybody," Mike Turkki reassured me. "But he does pull weird pranks every once in a while."

Then thinking this would ease me, he told me about the night he heard the downstairs door open, close and then footsteps entering the production room. He bounded down the stairs to see who it was. Nobody was there.

Mike said that whenever he worked late, he felt like he was being watched.

"The hair stood up on the back of my neck," he said. "I didn't want to look but I had to. No one was ever there."

To add to my fears, production manager Darlene Havens told me that she used to hear Jack walking back and forth at night when she was pulling a night shift. The eerie thing was it was upstairs in an area nobody ever uses because it is so small.

Now, of course, I can say I have my own ghost stories.

One night, there was this strange smell. At first, I dismissed the smell as my imagination. I rationalized it by remembering that I had once read that some people, narcoleptics mainly, smell things before they faint. Maybe I was going to have a seizure. That seemed easier to believe than . . . a ghost. But I was not fooling myself. I knew.

Later that week, I was the only one in the building. It was noon. I was downstairs and heard a rustling of paper. I ran upstairs, muttering under my breath about editors that left their windows open with their desk full of paper. When I got there, paper was blown all about, but no window was open. I looked everywhere for the source of a breeze, none could be found.

I was so excited, I told everybody when they returned from lunch.

They just shrugged and simply said: "Jack's at it again."

This bulding was originally built for the B.C. Police Headquarters in about 1920 and was used by the RCMP. *It was later bought as a newspaper office and it is now owned by Cariboo Press which operates at* Lakes District News. *Photo by Cecile Phillips.*

As the story goes, Jack was a man who had actually died in the heritage home, now our office. He was incarcerated in the building when it served as the RCMP headquarters, jail and the staff sergeant's residence. For some reason, the distraught prisoner had hung himself in his cell. The story remains fully unsubstantiated. But a ghost does reside here.

In fact, a recent visit from the daughter of the last staff sergeant to live in the heritage building helps build up a case.

She was in town and wanted to look around her old home. It was fun accompanying her on the tour of the building, she telling us this was her bedroom, this was the kitchen, stuff like that. At the end of the tour, I had mustered my courage (prodded in the back by Darlene), to ask her if anything "er . . . supernatural" had occurred to them while they lived there.

A meaningful glance passed between her and a friend accompanying her. Then a torrent of unexplained events poured forth. Stereos turning on and off without aid, things being moved, footsteps at night, a pane of shattered glass in the middle of the basement.

Our guest felt "it" was particularly active when she was there because she was a pre-pubescent teen and poltergeists work their pranks through girls like that. She was convinced "it" was in fact poltergeist.

When she left, we took in a deep breath and then — well, we went back to work. After all, we were in the newspaper business. Makes for a good story but we can't believe in this stuff.

There is no such thing as ghosts...right?

—*Cecile Phillips*

FORT NELSON NEWS

 The *Fort Nelson News* is the province's most northerly newspaper and covers a region larger than Nova Scotia.

Founded by Margaret L. "Ma" Murray on October 24, 1959, the paper was sold to Bob Angus a year later and purchased by Tony and Judith Kenyon in 1974. The *News* has a net paid circulation of 2,500 and is distributed in Watson Lake, Fort Nelson, Alaska Highway, Fort Liard and Fort Simpson.

Fort Nelson has changed markedly during the past quarter of a century.

Ma Murray started the paper in response to a request from a few of the 600 or so residents of Fort Nelson intent upon creating a community after they purchased five-acre sites along the highway after the army vacated the land. One of those residents was Stella Mathews, a motel owner, who provided Ma with a table where she wrote copy, sold ads and stored her film. Ma's children, Georgina Keddel and George Murray, set the type, laid out the pages and loaded the bundles.

The crude production process was complete only after everything was stuffed in a large envelope and dispatched on the bus to Fort St. John.

Ma was in her seventieth year when she started the paper. After about a year she found a buyer — Bob Angus. He was a newspaperman from Vancouver who had arrived in Fort St. John to operate a cafe, but a fire curtailed that project. Rich with a $3,000 insurance cheque, Bob bought a trailer, a table, a typewriter, a camera and became the voice of the community. His slogan was "Watch Your Step Pardner, this country is loaded with opportunity."

Photo by Mike Thomas, Yukon News.

Bob was iconoclastic and perhaps saw a dream bigger than the reality of a dusty truck stop and motel strip. He encouraged many people, particularly professionals — teachers, doctors and lawyers — to share his dream. He also managed to spend most of the five months of winter (with frequent drops to -40 Celsius), outside the country, leaving the 12-page tabloid to any aspiring writer who might be passing through. An Australian pilot did the photography one winter, mainly party shots; a young woman who left the area to attend college in Japan wrote pages of correspondence about her experiences; a United Church minister's wife became a star attraction by creating local cartoons.

When Tony and Judith Kenyon and their four-year-old daughter arrived from London, England, Tony with a shiny new surgical degree, Bob Angus met them at the airport and said: "Dr. Kenyon, I presume."

When Angus asked Judith what she did for a living and learned she was a reporter he said: "Oh, you've been sent by God!"

This was a carefree time, taxes were low, businesses small, opportunity rife, and those who had good jobs came and went in two-year intervals. Like most northern communities, Fort Nelson's permanent residents were a mixture of native, Metis and an assortment of wanderers who had found the place amenable to their shortcomings. To a reporter it was meat and drink.

In the 1970s, Fort Nelson became a place where barges, highways, airports, railways and pipelines converged to coalesce into a regional centre for an area rich in resources. No sooner had this, Bob Angus' dream, been realized, when he came down with a rare disease and died.

After his death, his estate was sold and the Kenyons took over publishing. Since then, the *News*, now one of the oldest businesses in Fort Nelson, has seen much change. Soon after taking over the paper, the Kenyons decided to do away with Ma's techniques, including the large envelope. In its place, two blue Compugraphic typesetters arrived with layout boards. The *News* was now a proper newspaper, including a staff, a darkroom and deadlines.

The paper has always been sent at least 300 miles out for printing, first to Fort St. John, then Prince George and now to Dawson Creek.

The *News* has recorded all as the community has rapidly grown — from personal accounts of bear attacks, plane crashes and riverboat accidents to peculiar stories and regular day-to-day stuff.

There is something satisfying about the stories and the people in this region that brings new enthusiasm to the job of running a paper each week. And a good sign that readers are being properly served is evident in a strong subscriber base dating back 20 years — not many city papers can match that. The *Fort Nelson News* — published every week — with the ghosts of Ma and Bob very much a part of the operation.

FORT SAINT JAMES, THE CALEDONIA COURIER

 The roots of Fort St. James' weekly newspaper, *The Caledonia Courier*, can be traced back to the late 1960s.

On October 22, 1969, Bud and Ruth Hallock published the first edition of *The Courier*.

"We started with eight pages. We had to run the paper to Prince George (an hour and 40 minutes away) to get it printed," recalls Bud, who lives in Terrace.

"We typed the paper on a regular typewriter. I remember we had to type the thing three times to get it justified. It was very laborious."

The Hallocks started a newspaper in Fort St. James for one simple reason: the community needed one.

"Ruth had been an editor before at a paper in Langley," Bud says. "We had lived in Fort St. James before and decided to move back north and start the paper."

Bud and Ruth ran the paper for just over six years when they decided to sell, but kept it in the family.

Roper Knox, editor (on left) and Mark Warner, publisher.

Daughters Shelly and Laurie, and Shelly's friend Kathy Wraight, purchased *The Courier* in February 1976.

"Laurie and I made the original decision to buy the paper, that was one of our top priorities," Wraight says.

The women would stay at the helm for four years, until "they could no longer take any more scenic pictures of Stuart Lake."

"We had lost Laurie along the way and acquired another partner but the bottom line was we were suffering from burnout," Kathy says.

In 1980, Rick O'Connor bought *The Courier* and would run it for three years.

"We experimented with delivering both *The Courier* and the *Omineca Express* from Vanderhoof," O'Connor says from his office in Vancouver. "We tried that for a year but people in Fort St. James didn't want Vanderhoof news. They wanted *The Courier* to be Fort St. James-oriented."

O'Connor sold *The Courier* to the Cariboo Press chain in 1983. Today, *The Courier* remains part of Cariboo Press.

"We're still a weekly paper and we keep *The* Courier full of Fort St. James news," current editor Roger Knox explains. "The only time we print something from elsewhere is if it somehow impacts our town. And for a town of just over 2,000 people, there is always something going on. It's never really a problem filling the pages."

Mark Warner, who also oversees the *Omineca Express* and *Fraser Lake Bugle*, is the publisher of *The Courier*.

"*The Courier* averages 16-20 pages per week," he says. "Our subscription base in Fort St. James is now over 1,000. People in the community like our product."

The Courier is produced at the *Express* office in Vanderhoof, and then is shipped to Williams Lake for printing. It is driven back for distribution, through the post office or retail outlets, on Wednesdays.

KITIMAT NORTHERN SENTINEL

 For anyone writing a history of Kitimat, the back issues of the *Northern Sentinel* would be vital to their research.

That is because the newspaper has been there almost since the beginning.

Wind Blasting by Mike Thomas, Yukon News.

Howard T. Mitchell founded the paper in 1954, when Alcan's aluminum smelter had yet to hit full stride and the potential readership was limited to a couple of thousand construction workers and a mere dozen permanent-resident families.

The two-pager was produced on a 19x24 offset press, which was housed in a 12 by 18-foot shack whose earlier occupant had been a diesel power plant.

The all-male staff bunked down in another plywood shack, but could take some consolation from its picturesque location — right next to a mountain-fed creek complete with waterfall.

In keeping with the multi-national make-up of Kitimat — a characteristic that has not changed — the first editor was an Australian, Ken Bromley, an articulate individual who became everyone's friend.

In those early days the *Sentinel* was something of a "tourist attraction," visitors to the smelter construction project being taken to gaze through the windows of what the guide described as "a great future daily newspaper in earliest embryo." A somewhat grandiose description, to be sure, but grandiose was the common currency in those days of heady optimism.

A couple of years after the *Sentinel's* inception, Kitimat took the big step away from being a collection of bunk houses and rudimentary homes huddled around the smelter. Construction of the townsite began, which included development of both residential neighbourhoods and the City Centre, the commercial hub of this much-planned city-in-the-making.

Sadly, when it came to the City Centre, the *Sentinel* was not invited to the party. The master plan designated "dirty industries" such as a newspaper to the Service Centre, safely located out of sight and hearing on the other side of the river from the city proper. The *Sentinel* remains at that location today, where a building was constructed, complete with a flat-bed web perfecting press, three Linotypes plus job printing and lithographic equipment necessary to a self-contained newspaper and commercial printing plant.

A lot has happened in the 45 years since the first *Sentinel* was printed. The city grew with the addition of a pulp and paper mill in the early 70s and a methanol plant in the early 80s and the paper kept pace.

By the late 80s the *Northern Sentinel* was coming out three times a week and serving both Kitimat and Terrace. Howard T. Mitchell had also started up the *Hazelton Sentinel* and *Stewart Sentinel*, both printed in Kitimat. Given that the Stewart copy and photos were delivered by a bus negotiating a less than perfect "highway," winter editions of that paper were always somewhat iffy.

Howard Mitchell died in 1990 and his son Howard took over the publishing duties. Shortly thereafter, the Hazelton and Stewart papers were laid to rest.

As for the *Northern Sentinel*, it eventually pulled out of Terrace to concentrate on its home community with a Wednesday subscription edition and a Saturday freebie.

On November 1, 1995, the *Sentinel* changed hands when Mitchell Press sold the operation to Cariboo Press. The immediate effect of that was a consolidation of the Saturday product: Cariboo Press's *Terrace Standard* had been sending a Saturday freebie into Kitimat since shortly after its arrival on the scene in 1988.

And the *Sentinel* changed its look in May 1997 when a readership survey indicated readers preferred a tabloid format.

Today the Wednesday *Sentinel* goes out to 2,500 subscribers and the joint effort Saturday *Weekend Advertiser* is distributed to nearly 16,000 homes from Kitimat to Terrace to the Hazeltons, Stewart and even as far north as Dease Lake. Northern Sentinel Press also continues to meet the commercial printing needs of the community.

As a community, Kitimat has not, and never will, reach the lofty projections of a population of 50,000 as put forward by the original planners. However, it enjoys a standard of services unrivalled in the province because of the lucrative tax base local industries provide. Plus a jewel-like setting where the salty expanse of the Douglas Channel, dark and silent forests and alpine meadows are all just minutes away from the centre of town.

And that is the way we like it.

—*Malcolm Baxter*

PRINCE GEORGE FREE PRESS

First, there was the empty office that had to be filled with people and computers and turned into something that resembled a newsroom.

Then there were the contacts that needed to be made and the selling of ads, writing of stories, taking of pictures.

Finally, there was the putting it all together into one cohesive package. And it all had to be done yesterday.

Months of preparation had culminated in a frantic 30-hour grind past deadline getting one of B.C.'s newest community papers out.

And there it was. The *Prince George Free Press* hit the streets — literally — on November 2, 1994.

The year's first snow began falling just as unprotected bundles of the paper were dropped of at the impromptu distribution centre — the parking lot across from the *Free Press* office.

Wet papers started getting wetter with the brewing storm and there were not enough drivers to get the paper out.

Shane Mills, the paper's founding editor, recalls driving in the middle of a blizzard through a town he'd only lived in for a month looking for street addresses as he and sportswriter Jim Swanson helped deliver the inaugural issue.

The *Free Press* was launched.

The *Prince George Free Press* is still new enough to remember those early days, the days when the conviction that we were doing something good, something right, sometimes overruled common sense.

What we were doing mattered. To hell with futurists and naysayers, Mr. Mills set out with a simple vision. "It's a newspaper's job to print the news and raise hell."

The *Free Press* has raised hell for a mere four years. But in that time it has managed to grow from its origins as a modest weekly paper to a meaty twice-weekly that has taken the newspaper community by storm.

It has collected a number of BCYCNA and CCNA awards since its first year of eligibility, the highlight coming just three years into the life of the paper when it was voted Canada's best community newspaper in the largest circulation class at the 1997 CCNA awards.

Staff has almost doubled, a mailroom has been added, some faces have changed. However, the attitude has not altered.

Every issue of the *Free Press* entwines the paper with Prince George as it chronicles the city's history in the making.

They say a newspaper is history on the run. We do not make history; we record it.

Fifty years from now, when the next edition of the BCYCNA history book hits the shelves, this story will be the same.

PRINCE GEORGE THIS WEEK

 As it moves toward its second decade, *Prince George This Week* continues to grow and expand in its market.

Created in the fall of 1989 to supplement the daily *Prince George*

Citizen's coverage, *Prince George This Week* has grown into a thriving, award-winning publication.

Originally delivered as a supplement with the Wednesday *Citizen*, *This Week* moved to Sundays in 1994, taking on its own delivery system and another measure of independence in the process. Early in its existence, the paper found its wings and made slow but steady strides. Coupled with a sister publication, a successful classified paper called the *Central Interior Buy and Sell*, the

paper carved out a niche for itself in the growing Prince George market.

The last four years, however, have seen the paper take giant steps, firmly embedding itself into the community's focus. Increased sectionalization of the editorial content in late 1994 allowed *This Week* to focus more on the people of the community it served. A 12 1/2-inch tab since its inception, the paper dropped the magazine-style, full-page front-page photo in favour of a newsier front page. The opinion section was expanded from one page to two.

Over time, the paper's niche became clearer. Faced with two other publications in the same market, both of which have greater frequency, *Prince George This Week* has taken on the mandate of a true community newspaper. There is a greater emphasis on telling stories about the people who live in the community, thus giving a snapshot of what kind of city Prince George really is.

In 1996, *Prince George This Week* expanded its mandate, beginning the publication of a quarterly magazine, the *Central Interior Business Magazine*.

The following year, the paper underwent a complete redesign. A cleaner look, with a new mast and more opportunity for full-process colour photos gave the paper an increased presence in a competitive community. It was split from one section to two in the same redesign. Later the same year, the staff moved, literally down the alley, from an over-sized building on Victoria Street to a cozy, renovated space across the street from their daily cousins.

In late 1997, the market expanded again — sort of. For a city of 75,000, Prince George covers a relatively large geographic area. So, *Prince George This Week* began targeting the communities within the larger community. In October of 1997, the *Hart Gazette*, a monthly community newspaper serving the city's residents north of the Nechako River, was launched.

As the newspaper has grown, so has its appeal. *This Week* has earned mention at both the BCYCNA and the CCNA awards in recent years, taking home hardware in a broad range of categories. Through this change, however, has been stability. All but a couple of staff members have left the paper since its inception.

In a changing world, though, remaining static is the first step toward oblivion. So there is no doubt that more growth is in the offing for *Prince George This Week*.

—*Tim Renneberg*

QUESNEL CARIBOO OBSERVER

From the edition which was published on August 29, 1908 to the modern twice-weekly publications, the *Quesnel Cariboo Observer* has provided continuous community content.

In the beginning subscriptions were $2 a year, and advertising cost 25 cents an inch. The first publisher, J.B. Daniell, promised that the paper would promote the Cariboo District as the area progressed and increased in population. It was suggested that the paper had been created to handle the real estate and land notice business generated by the 1908 Cariboo land boom. The first issue of the *Observer* contained four pages.

On its first anniversary, the paper was still going strong. In the August 21, 1909 edition, a petition urging the government to keep motor cars off Cariboo roads was printed.

The March 19, 1910 issue of the *Observer* was printed on wrapping paper as the white paper that had been ordered did not arrive. Daniell noted that all the wrapping paper available in Quesnel had been scrounged to put out the paper.

On January 23, 1911 the *Observer* was sold to Albert Dollemmayer and by January 28 had acquired the editor it would have for the next 23 years, John G. Hutchcroft.

Hutchcroft had originally come to Quesnel to edit the *Quesnel Times* but only one edition was ever printed. He then began working for the *Quesnel Observer*.

Difficult times ensued when the government reserved the land in the Cariboo, thus ending the land boom. With revenues drastically reduced, Hutchcroft's boss decided to "sever relations with the community," putting him out of a job.

On August 4, 1911, Edward Kepner, owner of Quesnel's Occidental Hotel, bought the *Observer*, retaining Hutchcroft.

By the paper's 25th anniversary it averaged six pages a week with subscriptions still at $2 per year. Starting in the early 1920s Hutchcroft's son, Bev, worked on the paper. By 1934, when John Hutchcroft died at the age of 67, the *Cariboo Observer* had begun to look more like the modern conception of a newspaper with a front-page photograph, different typefaces and styles of headlines and editorials set on two-column type. It contained an average of eight pages per issue.

When William Griffith bought the paper in July 1949 he continued the *Observer* tradition.

"It is our firm conviction that a newspaper should be a true and faithful servant of the community," he wrote. Subscription costs rose to $3.50 per year by 1958. Griffith continued as editor and publisher until 1965 when it was purchased by Northwest Publications.

This newspaper chain operated the *Observer* for a scant four and a half years before the chain was dissolved and the newspapers sold.

On April 15, 1969 the paper was taken over by mill owner John Ernst.

The Ernst era lasted through to August of 1984 and saw changes in the community that included unprecedented industrial, commercial and population growth. In response, the *Observer* became a twice-weekly publication, issued on Tuesdays and Thursdays.

In 1984 David Black, president of Cariboo Press Ltd. in Williams Lake, purchased the *Observer*. The paper reverted to its weekly Wednesday publishing.

In December of 1984 one of the *Observer's* most memorable editors, Jerry MacDonald, took over.

Again, the focus of the community newspaper was preserved. MacDonald was a well-known figure at sports, political and social events.

As of this writing Pattie Paull publishes the Cariboo *Observer* and Neil Horner is the editor. The paper is published on Wednesday and Sunday. Throughout its 90-year history the *Quesnel Cariboo Observer* has maintained an abiding philosophy that community comes first. The newspaper is the record-keeper of the community history and takes pride in striving to maintain that perspective, objectivity and balance.

QUEEN CHARLOTTE ISLANDS OBSERVER

It all started during the snowy Christmas season of 1968, Mable and Doug Leached recalled. There was three feet of snow on the ground in Tlell and ice everywhere. Their eldest son, Ralph, was home for the holidays from high school in Prince George. The two younger boys, Tom and Richard, were out of Port Clements school for Christmas.

Who knows what would have happened had it not snowed so much that year. But the weather was so bad the family was stuck inside the house and they spent the time dreaming up all kinds of crazy ideas for things to do.

One was to start a brewery, which Doug wanted to call the Blithe Spirit Brewery. Another was to start a newspaper for the islands, which had been without one since the *Queen Charlotte Islands Advertiser*, published in Prince Rupert, had packed it in.

The newspaper idea was the one that stuck because Doug theorized that too many Islanders brewed their own beer for the brewery to be successful. Four months later, on May 1, 1969, the first issue of the *Queen Charlotte Islands Observer* hit the streets.

At this point, the Leaches had been living in Tlell for 10 years. They had moved there from the Lower Mainland where Doug had worked as a physiotherapist. They had no experience with newspapers except reading them and had hardly any equipment.

In fact, there was not even electricity in Tlell until the mid-70s. Doug and Mable bought a generator especially for their newspaper business. The first *Observers* were written on manual typewriters and printed on a duplicator. Ads and occasionally photographs were done on an old scanner. The two boys who were still at home, Tom and Richard, printed the paper in one of the bedrooms. Doug and Mable took the boys' half-size pool table, placed a pin-pong table on top of it and collated and stapled the *Observer* there every Wednesday. When it was finally done, they would deliver it to the Tlell Post Office, which was then located at the Richardson Ranch.

Mable remembers that Dorothy Richardson would wait up until midnight some Wednesday nights with the kettle boiling. Dorothy had a collection of all the community papers that had been published on the Charlottes and from these she would write the "Way Back When" column, which ran in early *Observers*.

The roads were hazardous in those days. The highway was not paved until the early 1970s. Doug and Mable drove regularly to Masset, which was then a booming village with two schools and an expanding military station. Doug remembers driving to Nadu in the middle of a heavy snowstorm and getting stuck. At that moment, the school bus from Masset came along. A bunch of school kids got out, picked the car right up off the ground and turned it around so it was facing Tlell and Doug could drive back.

After a couple of years printing the *Observer* in their house, Doug and Mable bought an 8 by 30-foot trailer from Al Porter and placed it near the highway, and that tiny trailer became the newspaper office. The duplicator was replaced by a small AB Dick press, which they put out in the chicken coop. Bob Crooks dropped by for a cup of tea one day and left with a job: he has been printing the Observer ever since.

The *Observer* did not have much of what Doug called "hard news." There were reports of meetings, news about businesses starting up or expanding, visiting dignitaries, births, deaths, weddings, court reports and fires.

"Items that constituted news more often than not were community halls and churches burning down," Doug says. Since he became editor, almost every community hall on the island has had a fire.

Most of the news came over the telephone or from people dropping by on their way through Tlell. Letters to the editor also formed a big part of the news.

The best story they ever came across was the one about the lost glass eye.

"Somebody brought in a glass eye they found on the road, so we put an ad in the paper. Found: glass eye," says Doug. "We figured someone would be in a bad way."

And someone who had lost their glass eye did show up at the *Observer* office to claim it. But it wasn't the right one.

"It was a right glass eye and theirs was a left one."

The story of the two glass eyes somehow made the news in England and France, Mable says. "It was unbelievable."

In 1978, Doug and Mable bought a 24-man bunkhouse from Juskatla and the boys hauled it into the field just north of their house, where it still stands today.

Mable and Doug sold the paper and retired in 1985. The new owners, Jeff and Dianne King, published the paper in Tlell until the *Observer* moved to its present location, on 5th Avenue in Queen Charlotte, in 1992.

SMITHERS, THE INTERIOR NEWS

Joseph L. Coyle founded *The Interior News* in 1909. Coyle first came to the Bulkley Valley by way of Juneau, Alaska, where he had been demonstrating the new Simplex typesetting machine. He liked the area and decided to settle.

His first edition was published in Aldermere, near the present site of Telkwa, about 10 miles from Smithers.

Many snags cropped up in the early days of the young newspaper, including the theft of the only typewriter in the plant. Delayed shipments of newsprint necessitated at least one issue going to press on white wrapping paper.

Coyle possessed the only paper cutter in town, so one of his chores was to cut sheets of money into bills for the newly-appointed Aldermere Bank.

When Aldermere faded out of existence, Coyle moved *The Interior News* to Smithers, setting up shop there in 1913.

Eagle Landing by Mike Thomas, Yukon News.

At around the same time, Coyle invented a new type of egg carton for transporting eggs. This carton proved very successful, and in 1919 Coyle moved to Vancouver to start manufacturing cartons on a much wider basis.

He therefore sold *The News* to L.B. Warner in 1919, and the paper was controlled and operated by the Warner family until it was taken over by North Central Press Ltd. in 1968.

Through its formative years from 1969 onward, the company saw such people as Gary White involved, along with Bill Yorke-Hardy, a former Smithers businessman and mining entrepreneur. During the late '70s Keith Marshall became the principal shareholder and guided the paper through rapid growth with the addition of new typesetting equipment, a press and an expansion in quarters, plus constant circulation growth throughout the west-central region of B.C..

In the December 24, 1979 issue of the paper, Keith Marshall announced the sale of *The News* to Cariboo Press Ltd., publishers of the *Williams Lake Tribune*. They stated that with "the advent of new technologies and the need to consider these in the light of equipment requirements and production techniques, the sale of the paper will provide a stronger base from which to meet the challenges of the future."

Cariboo Press owner David Black says of the purchase, "*The Interior News* has always been a fine paper and I hope to continue with its excellence in publication. A newspaper must not only reflect the life of the community but must also help boost its aims and directions. It must also serve the role of critic at times and, where necessary, give leadership. It is my sincere hope that the community will continue in its tradition of participation in *The Interior News* and will stay involved as intently as it has in the past".

Since taking over *The Interior News*, Cariboo Press has continually upgraded equipment to meet changing technology, a move that eventually led to removing the press and having the paper printed in the main plant in Williams Lake. This allowed for more colour and page capacity. In the past seven years, the old Compugraphic equipment has been replaced with state-of-the-art ad composition computers. In 1998, the transition to "digital" darkroom was made.

Bruce Busby became the first general manager under Cariboo Press in 1980. In October 1984 Cheryl Mercer was appointed publisher. Cheryl moved to Smithers from Nanaimo where she had worked with the *Nanaimo Free Press*. Linda Patry took over from Cheryl in September 1988. In July 1991 the current publisher, Vic Swan, moved from the *Sidney Review* to assume the role of publisher of *The Interior News* and regional manager for Cariboo Press newspapers in the north.

TERRACE STANDARD

Every so often somebody asks us what kind of wire service — the term for a system that delivers stories to newspapers — we use.

We do not have a wire service.

The *Terrace Standard* is a classic community newspaper, concerned solely with publishing items of interest about and for the area it serves. We have done that for the past 10 years, since our first issue hit the streets in April 1988.

As is the case with other community newspapers, we are divided into three categories — a section for hard news, editorials, features and letters to the editor, a community section for stories on people and community events and a section for local sports.

It is not an easy job to gather the events of one week and place them within the confines of such a product, which is then delivered to stores and homes.

However, it is a rewarding one.

The satisfaction comes from people reading an article and then saying, "I never knew that."

And we look forward to receiving telephone calls and letters to the editor from people either commenting on what they've read or telling us we've done a poor job. That is because it is our readers who ultimately make up the newspaper and without them, we would not be here.

Yet there is much more to a newspaper's life than the news because the newsroom makes up just one element of what is involved in putting out each week's issue.

We have a business office, a circulation section, a production staff that assembles the jigsaw puzzle of stories, photographs and ads. We also have a sales section of advertising representatives and their ad makers, which is in daily contact with our advertisers who use the newspaper as a vital and valuable tool for their own business success.

Without the valuable and constant efforts of each of the above, the eternal demands of meeting deadlines simply could not be met.

Equally as important is the small army of newspaper carriers who faithfully cover their routes each week and the people who deliver the bundles of newspapers to them.

The *Terrace Standard* has been fortunate to take part in and to witness the greatest decade of growth in the history of Terrace and the northwest.

The growth in cultural, recreational, educational and transportation services and of different kinds of housing has been phenomenal.

We have covered land claims — the single largest social, economic and political challenge facing the northwest. We have covered the difficulties of the economy, we have told stories of important people and of interesting characters. We have covered happy events and we have covered tragedy and sorrow. In addition, we have tried to do it all within the goal of letting the community know about itself.

Our job is to keep doing that for the next decade and beyond.

VALEMOUNT/MCBRIDE, THE VALLEY SENTINEL

A reporter from a big-city newspaper stopped to visit with a friend who operated a little country weekly. He asked his friend, "How can you keep up your circulation in a town where everyone knows what everyone else is doing?"

The editor grinned and said: "They know what everyone else is doing all right, but they read the paper to see who's been caught at it!"

— *Excerpt from The Valley Echo humour column, September 18, 1963.*

The Robson Valley, with two major highways running through it, does not seem especially isolated. Before the highways were constructed in the late 1960s and early 1970s, however, contact with larger centres was somewhat limited. Despite the fact that people in the small settlements of McBride, Valemount, Tete Jaune Cache, Mount Robson, Dunster, Lamming Mills and Croyden seemed to know the business of each other, a community newspaper played an important role in keeping a sense of togetherness.

James Mewhort started the first paper in the Robson Valley in McBride. Mewhort, a native of England, began publishing in April 1914. His paper, called the *McBride Bulletin*, was printed on the Main Street of McBride. Another paper, dubbed *The Quill*, was also printed in McBride in the 1930s.

In 1957, *The Valley Echo* came into existence. It was stationed in

McBride and had a McBride editor, but the copy was made up of submissions from all over the Robson Valley. *The Valley* Echo and its predecessors were seen to be serving one cohesive community, rather than several small separate ones.

"Living in the Robson Valley was like living on an island," explains longtime McBride resident Marilyn Wheeler, of the time before the highways were constructed. "You could drive to the larger places like Jasper or Kamloops in the summer, but the roads were questionable even then." McBride's nearest village neighbour was Valemount, located 100 kilometres to the south.

The Valley Echo, which was printed in Tofield, Alberta, sold for seven cents a copy.

The next paper to grace the valley was *The Robson Valley Echo*, which started in 1962. This paper was again based in McBride.

When the highways were built, Valemount, a logging and railway town, began to grow and wanted its independence from McBride, which was supported by agriculture as well as logging and the railway.

In 1969, the *Robson Valley Courier* was started in McBride and, in 1972, *The Canoe Mountain Echo* was started in Valemount. Both papers were published by Pyramid Press Limited in Jasper, Alberta. The *Robson Valley Courier* had a circulation of 850 and *The Canoe Mountain* Echo, 650. Each paper cost 15 cents per copy. The name of *The Canoe Mountain Echo* came from a contest run by Fred Donovan, the publisher. In the first issue of the paper, three big question marks were shown where the banner was supposed to be. People in the community submitted names and the chosen one was displayed on each subsequent issue.

Though the two main villages in the Robson Valley were separating and their respective papers growing more sophisticated, they still gave the impression of having a very intimate and familiar relationship with their readers. Readers who had a complaint regarding the paper would quickly discover the editor was a person with feelings.

In 1976, Barbara Shepherd, editor of *The Canoe Mountain Echo*, received an anonymous letter criticizing the paper for not covering an event. The letter quickly became the subject of that week's editorial: "Well, dear 'Perturbed,' unless someone has the sense to phone or tell me when something is happening, there's about as much chance of me knowing about it as there is me knowing 'Perturbed's' real name . . . So wake up, I'm only the editor. I need your help if you want a good newspaper . . ."

The editor of the *Robson Valley Courier*, too, tried to keep a light-hearted attitude toward human error in the paper.

In 1976, editor Sadie Frye told her readers: "If you find mistakes in this publication, please consider they are there for a purpose. We publish something for everyone, and some people are always looking for mistakes!"

The 19-year reign of Pyramid Press ended in 1988. At this time, Black Tusk Holdings Limited purchased *The Valley Sentinel*, a Valemount publication owned by Mureen Brownlee, and the Valemount publication owned by Maureen Brownlee and eliminated the Pyramid Press publications in McBride and Valemount. Brownlee was subsequently employed as the publisher and editor of *The Valley Sentinel*, which covered news in the whole valley.

Maureen Brownlee ran the *Sentinel* for the next six years, during which time her company, Lesli Ventures, purchased the paper back from Black Tusk Holdings.

In September 1994, Brownlee sold *The Valley Sentinel* to Bill and Rena Mahoney, a couple from Tete Jaune Cache. The Mahoneys, now under their company name of Whitehorn Publishing Limited, have operated *The Valley Sentinel* for the past four years. The paper still covers the entire Robson Valley, with reporters employed in both Valemount and McBride.

—*Kyla Hoogers*

VANDERHOOF, OMINECA EXPRESS-FRASER LAKE BUGLE

On June 7, 1978 the first-ever edition of the *Omineca Express-Fraser Lake Bugle* was produced. The originator, Rick O'Connor, has since gone on to bigger things but has not forgotten that date. Indeed, when I called him to learn more about the paper's history, it was the first thing he told me.

O'Connor came to Vanderhoof in 1976 to work at CI Radio. One day, while out selling advertising, some merchants told him they were unhappy with the then reigning newspaper.

The *Nechako Chronicle* had served the area for a long and illustrious period but was evidently on its last legs.

O'Connor asked the merchants if they would support his efforts to start up a newspaper of his own. When the answer was yes the work began.

"I sold my car, bought some computer equipment and started the paper," O'Connor says.

Because it was completely new to them, O'Connor and his partner, Katherine Henley, pulled two all-nighters to get the first issue out.

Originally it was called the *Omineca Advertiser*, and while there was some news in it, it was intended to be nothing more than a shopper.

However, readers liked the style of writing and were soon clamouring for more news. O'Connor knew he was on to something good when they turned a small profit in the second month.

For the first year and a half, the *Express* was given away free. When they switched to paid, 80 per cent of those who received the *Express* became subscribers.

Even so, for the first couple of years O'Connor and Henley worked seven days a week, taking one week a year off for holidays.

"We didn't hire that many staff in the first couple of years because we couldn't really afford them," O'Connor says.

O'Connor also came up with placing the Fraser Lake news in a separate section instead of burying it in the back of the *Express*.

He also oversaw the editorial side while a succession of reporters went through the doors. Possibly the most memorable, he says, was Cary Rodin, who is now a lawyer in Victoria.

The biggest story during O'Connor's five years here was the Kemano Completion Project and how Alcan should be allowed to use water from the Nechako River.

"I think we filled up a whole filing cabinet with papers and briefs," he says. "There wasn't a week that went by without something about Kemano."

Only 30 years old, O'Connor decided to sell the *Express* in 1983 at the same time the current owner, David Black, was on a buying spree.

Black's Cariboo Press had been printing the *Express* since day one, and with his focus on community weeklies it seemed natural that he would want the newspaper.

O'Connor moved on to Quesnel when the paper was sold.

Since then, the *Express* has gone through its share of publishers and editors. Publishers of note include Irene Swan and Brian Borle. Mark Warner is the current publisher.

Of course, Vanderhoof has grown and so has the *Express*. Some things never change, however. The debate over Alcan and the Nechako still gets headlines and local merchants continue to value the *Express*, now a paper with a 20-year history.

Williams Lake Tribune

Williams Lake is a young town in an old setting. By the mid-1880s, the future of the original town seemed assured. Here the new stipendiary magistrate for the Cariboo had made headquarters. There was a flour mill, sawmill and British Columbia's first distillery. All that was needed was the approaching Cariboo Highway. Then disaster struck.

The road bypassed the settlement. The courthouse was abandoned, the post office moved to Barkerville, and the valley was left to sleep for 50 years until another mode of transportation was established.

In 1919 rails of the Pacific Great Eastern (now British Columbia Railway) reached the townsite and surveyors were already at work laying out streets and lots in the wheat fields.

In 1929, Williams Lake was incorporated as a village and, one year later, in October 1930, the first issue of the *Williams Lake Tribune* appeared. Editor and proprietor was the late E.P. Cotton, a printer by trade. The eight-page issues of the day consisted of six pages of boilerplate with two pages reserved for local news. If local news and advertising were particularly heavy, a single sheet would be made up and inserted.

The newspaper was operated by Mr. Cotton for 10 years and in 1940 was sold to Chilcotin rancher George Washington Renner, who moved to the Cariboo from the United States in 1918. His decision to buy the newspaper probably stemmed from his deep interest in politics and during his tenure he was actively engaged in Liberal party work.

Adam Killick, Yukon News.

Gradually the boilerplate became wholly "home print."

In January 1950 ownership of the newspaper again changed, with Clive Stangoe starting his long association with the *Tribune*. At the time, he was the youngest publisher in the province and he was the first publisher of the *Tribune* with editorial experience.

The *Tribune* became recognized for its editorial content and general typographical appearance — something successive publishers and editors have striven to maintain. The *Tribune* has won more than 90 provincial and national awards.

In the late 1960s Stangoe sold the newspaper to Northwest Publications and continued as publisher. Then in 1969 Northwest Publications put the newspaper up on the block. Alan Black, then an executive with Northwest, suggested to Stangoe that they go into partnership and buy the paper. Stangoe agreed and a deal was made that same day. A couple of years later, in 1972, the decision was made to go twice-weekly. The broadsheet has published twice a week since then.

In the mid-70s Alan Black's son David purchased the newspaper and began building the Cariboo Press chain. Black now lives in Victoria and retains ownership. The Cariboo Press head office, however, remains in Williams Lake. Bob Grainger, who served as publisher of the *Tribune* in the 1980s, is now president of Cariboo Press. Born and raised in Williams Lake, the current publisher is Gary Crosina.

In 1989, the *Tribune* launched a weekend shopper called *The Sunday Shopper*. It was created to counteract a competing "good news" newspaper operating in the city. In 1995 the Sunday shopper was changed to a tabloid and renamed *The Weekender*. While its competition has since folded, the *Weekender* and its parent newspaper, the *Tribune*, continue to thrive.

The *Tribune* now employs 75 full and part-time workers.

—Bill Phillips

YUKON NEWS

Ken Shortt had a dream. He wanted to run a newspaper in one of the world's most competitive regions. But his competition was not another newspaper, although the *Yukon Star* was tough to beat: it was the Yukon itself. The shear complexity of serving readers in an area this large seemed insurmountable. How do you reach them, and not in a geographical sense, but a journalistic one? Ken Shortt began his quest of discovery in 1960 when he founded the *Yukon News*, nee the *Advertiser*.

"Everybody told me I was nuts," says Shortt. "Perhaps I was. But the minute someone tells me it can't be done, that's when I know I have to do it."

Those first years few years were risky for Shortt. He kept a full-time job in the day and poured all his money and spare time putting together the paper at night. By 1965, he believed it was time to expand from weekly to daily, but he was at a loss over how to do it; after all, there were only so many hours in the day and dollars in the bank. When a guy named Dave Robertson showed up offering to work for nothing just to learn the newspaper business, Shortt jumped at the chance and the two became partners.

Dave Robertson was an ex-army officer, a building contractor and one-time editor of a university student newspaper. With his help, Shortt's dream of running a daily came true within a year. The *Yukon News* was the first daily in the north — the momentous occasion was celebrated in *Time* magazine.

"We produced a good newspaper," says Robertson. "But we still had to deal with our competition, the *Yukon Star*, which was entrenched in people's minds as the only local paper. Making them switch was not easy."

The *Yukon Daily News* never became a huge success. And the business relationship between Shortt and Robertson was not perfect. Before too long, Robertson was back at work as a contractor and Shortt was trying to run a daily paper on his own. By the late 1960s, the *Yukon News* switched back to being a weekly and started to profit again. But Shortt was exhausted. For 10 years, he had put his heart and soul into the publication, along with a printing company and a monthly magazine. It was time to sell.

In no time, Shortt's *Yukon News* was purchased by a group of businessmen.

"It was like giving up my own baby," says Shortt. "It was really, really tough."

But Shortt's mourning period would not last long. The buyers had no experience in the newspaper business. They were unable to continue the kind of success Shortt managed. The businessmen gave up and Shortt was compelled to buy the newspaper back from them.

"I just could not sit back and watch it fold," he says. So he spent all his savings and time to rebuild the paper. After a couple of years, he was ready to let go of his baby again and who should want to purchase but his old partner Dave Robertson.

Robertson's strategy for the *Yukon News'* future was simple.

"In my opinion, it was a matter of content," says Robertson. "Doing good, solid journalism would attract more readers."

Whatever it was Robertson did, it worked. The paper built up a strong readership and by 1986 its circulation finally surpassed the Star's.

"The key to success can be attributed to the people married to the advertisers," says Robertson half seriously. If the spouse of an advertiser likes the paper, the advertiser treats it like a mini market survey and puts his money where his partner's mouth is.

Thanks to the advertisers, or their wives and husbands, the *Yukon News* began to make a good and regular profit.

"It was quite a relief to know I could actually make my mortgage payments every month," admitted Robertson. "And there was a brief temptation to go hog-wild and buy a new building and new equipment, but I stopped myself."

In 1989, Robertson sold the business to his son Steven who, Robertson proudly boasts, managed to give the paper an even better reputation.

"They keep winning awards for design and journalism." And if the Robertson theory of newspaper success works, this second-generation Robertson may very well establish a long and prosperous future for the *Yukon News*.

Appendix

British Columbia   Community Newspaper Circulation 1,939,377

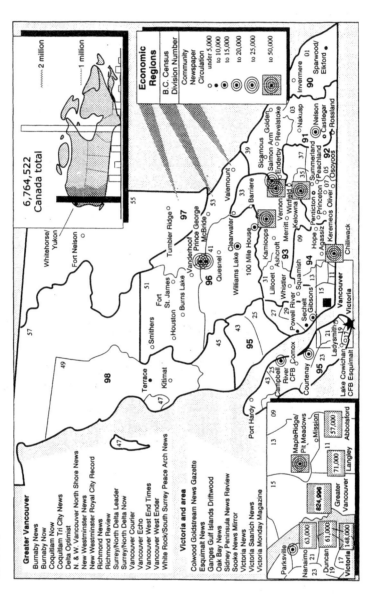

6,764,522
Canada total

2 million
1 million

Economic Regions

B.C. Census Division Number

Community Newspaper Circulation
- under 5,000
- to 10,000
- to 15,000
- to 20,000
- to 25,000
- to 50,000

Greater Vancouver
Burnaby News
Burnaby Now
Coquitlam Now
Coquitlam Tri City News
Delta Optimist
N. & W. Vancouver North Shore News
New Westminster News
New Westminster Royal City Record
Richmond News
Richmond Review
Surrey/North Delta Leader
Surrey/North Delta Now
Vancouver Courier
Vancouver Echo
Vancouver West End Times
Vancouver West Ender
White Rock/South Surrey Peace Arch News

Victoria and area
Colwood Goldstream News Gazette
Esquimalt News
Ganges Gulf Islands Driftwood
Oak Bay News
Sidney Peninsula News Review
Sooke News Mirror
Victoria News
Victoria Saanich News
Victoria Monday Magazine

100 MILE FREE HOUSE FREE PRESS
Box 459 #3 Pinkney Complex
160 Horse Lake Road
100 Mile House, BC, V0K 2E0
Tel: 250-395-2219
Fax: 250-395-3939

ABBOTSFORD NEWS
34375 Cyril St.
Abbotsford, BC, V2S 2H5
Tel: 604-853-1144
Fax: 604-850-5426

ABBOTSFORD TIMES
30887 Peardonville Road
Abbotsford, BC, V2T 6K2
Tel: 604-854-5244
Fax: 604-854-1140

AGASSIZ HARRISON OBSERVER
Box 129 #3 - 7092 Pioneer Ave.
Agassiz, BC, V0M 1A0
Tel: 604-796-2022
Fax: 604-796-2081

ALDERGROVE STAR
3089 272 St.
Aldergrove, BC, V4W 3R9
Tel: 604-856-8303
Fax: 604-856-5212

ARMSTRONG ADVERTISER
Box 610 3400 Okanagan St.
Armstrong, BC, V0E 1B0
Tel: 250-546-3121
Fax: 250-546-3636

ASHCROFT CACHE CREEK JOURNAL
Box 190 402 - 4th St.
Ashcroft, BC, V0K 1A0
Tel: 250-453-2261
Fax: 250-453-9625

BARRIERE N. THOMPSON STAR/JOURNAL
Box 1020 359 Borthwick Ave.
Barriere, BC, V0E 1E0
Tel: 250-672-5611
Fax: 250-672-9900

BELLA COOLA COAST MOUNTAIN NEWS
Box 250 (McKenzie Hwy)
Hagensborg, BC, V0T 1H0
Tel: 250-982-2696
Fax: 250-982-2512

BOWEN ISLAND UNDERCURRENT
Box 130 Government Road
Bowen Island, BC, V0N 1G0
Tel: 604-947-2442
Fax: 604-947-0148

BURNABY NEWS LEADER
6569 Kingsway
Burnaby, BC, V5E 1E1
Tel: 604-438-6397
Fax: 604-438-9699

BURNABY NOW
205A-3430 Brighton Ave.
Burnaby, BC, V5A 3H4
Tel: 604-444-3451
Fax: 604-444-3460

BURNS LAKE DISTRICT NEWS
Box 309 23 Third Ave.
Burns Lake, BC, V0J 1E0
Tel: 250-692-7526
Fax: 250-692-3685

CAMPBELL RIVER COURIER-ISLANDER
Box 310 1040 Cedar St.
Campbell River, BC, V9W 5B5
Tel: 250-287-7464
Fax: 250-287-8891

**CAMPBELL RIVER MIRROR /
NORTH ISLAND WEEKENDER**
Box 459 104 - 250 Dogwood St.
Campbell River, BC, V9W 2X9
Tel: 250-287-9227
Fax: 250-287-3238

CASTLEGAR SUN
465 Columbia Ave.
Castlegar, BC, V1N 1G3
Tel: 250-365-5266
Fax: 250-365-7762

CHETWYND ECHO
Box 750 Suite 215 5021 - 49th Ave.
Chetwynd, BC, V0C 1J0
Tel: 250-788-2246
Fax: 250-788-9988

CHILLIWACK PROGRESS
45860 Spadina Ave.
Chilliwack, BC, V2P 6H9
Tel: 604-702-5500
Fax: 604-792-4936

CHILLIWACK TIMES
102 - 45951 Tretheway Ave.
Chilliwack, BC, V2P 1K4
Tel: 604-792-9117
Fax: 604-792-9300

**CLEARWATER NORTH THOMPSON
TIMES**
Box 2592 Brooksfield Mall RR#1
63 Lodge Rd.
Clearwater, BC, V0E 1N0
Tel: 250-674-3343
Fax: 250-674-3410

**COLWOOD GOLDSTREAM
GAZETTE**
Box 7310 Depot D 839
117-777 Goldstream Ave.
Victoria, BC, V9B 5B7
Tel: 250-478-9552
Fax: 250-478-6545

COMOX TOTEM TIMES
CFB Comox
Lazo, BC, V0R 2K0
Tel: 250-339-2541
Fax: 250-339-5209

COQUITLAM NOW
#1 - 2700 Barnet Hwy
Coquitlam, BC, V3B 1B8
Tel: 604-942-4192
Fax: 604-464-4977

COQUITLAM TRI-CITY NEWS
1405 Broadway St.
Port Coquitlam, BC, V3C 6L6
Tel: 525-6397
Fax: 944-0703

**COURTENAY COMOX VALLEY
ECHO**
407-D Fifth St.
Courtenay, BC, V9N 1J7
Tel: 250-334-4722
Fax: 250-334-3172

**COURTENAY COMOX VALLEY
RECORD**
Box 3729 765 McPhee Ave.
Courtenay, BC, V9N 7P1
Tel: 250-338-5811
Fax: 250-338-5568

**CRANBROOK EAST KOOTENAY
WEEKLY**
822 Cranbrook St North
Cranbrook, BC, V1C 3R9
Tel: 250-426-5201
Fax: 732-3961

**CRANBROOK KOOTENAY
ADVERTISER**
1510 Second St. North
Cranbrook, BC, V1C 3L2
Tel: 250-489-3455
Fax: 250-489-3743

CRESTON VALLEY ADVANCE
Box 1279 115 - 10th Ave.
Creston, BC, V0B 1G0
Tel: 250-428-2266
Fax: 250-732-3961

DAWSON CREEK MIRROR
1316 Alaska Ave
Dawson Creek, BC, V1G 1Z3
Tel: 250-782-9424
Fax: 250-782-9454

DAWSON CREEK REGIONAL ADVERTISER
901 - 100th Ave.
Dawson Creek, BC, V1G 1W2
Tel: 250-782-4888
Fax: 250-732-3961

DELTA OPTIMIST
5485 48th Ave.
Delta, BC, V4K 1X2
Tel: 604-946-4451
Fax: 604-946-5680

DUNCAN CITIZEN
Box 158 469 Whistler St.
Duncan, BC, V9L 4X5
Tel: 250-748-2666
Fax: 250-732-3961

DUNCAN NEWS LEADER
2742 James St.
Duncan, BC, V9L 2X9
Tel: 250-746-4471
Fax: 250-748-1552

DUNCAN PICTORIAL
2742 James St.
Duncan, BC, V9L 2X9
Tel: 250-746-4471
Fax: 250-746-8529

ELK VALLEY EXTRA
Bag 5000 342 Second Ave.
Fernie, BC, V0B 1M0
Tel: 250-423-4666
Fax: 250-732-3961

ENDERBY COMMONER
Box 850 601A Cliff Ave
Enderby, BC, V0E 1V0
Tel: 250-838-7229
Fax: 250-838-7801

ESQUIMALT LOOKOUT
CFB Esquimalt
Box 17000 Station Forces
Victoria (FMO), BC, V9A 7N2
Tel: 250-385-0313
Fax: 250-361-3512

ESQUIMALT NEWS
1824 Store St.
Victoria, BC, V8T-4R4
Tel: 250-381-5664
Fax: 250-386-2624

FERNIE FREE PRESS
Bag 5000 342 Second Ave.
Fernie, BC, V0B 1M0
Tel: 250-423-4666
Fax: 250-732-3961

FORT NELSON NEWS
Box 600 5004 52nd Ave. W.
Fort Nelson, BC, V0C 1R0
Tel: 250-774-2357
Fax: 250-774-3612

FORT ST. JAMES CALEDONIA COURIER
Box 1298 366 Stuart Drive.
Vanderhoof, BC, V0J 1P0
Tel: 250-996-8482
Fax: 250-996-7973

FORT ST. JOHN, ALASKA HIGHWAY NEWS
9916-98th St.
Fort St. John, BC, V1J 3T8
Tel: 250-785-5631
Fax: 250-785-3522

FORT ST. JOHN NORTHERNER
9908 101 Ave.
Fort St. John, BC, V1J 2B2
Tel: 250-785-2890
Fax: 250-732-3961

GABRIOLA SOUNDER
C56, Suite 17 RR#1
Gabriola Island, BC, V0R 1X0
Tel: 250-247-9337
Fax: 250-257-8147

GANGES, GULF ISLANDS DRIFTWOOD
328 Lower Ganges Road
Salt Spring Island, BC, V8K 2V3
Tel: 250-537-9933
Fax: 250-537-2613

GOLDEN STAR
Box 149 413A Ninth Ave.
Golden, BC, V0A 1H0
Tel: 250-344-5251
Fax: 250-344-7344

GOLD RIVER RECORD
Box 279 Gold River, BC, V0P 1G0
Tel: 250-283-2325
Fax: 250-283-2527

GRAND FORKS GAZETTE/ BOUNDARY BULLETIN
Box 700 7330 Second Ave.
Grand Forks, BC, V0H 1H0
Tel: 250-442-2191
Fax: 250-442-3336

GREENWOOD BOUNDARY CREEK TIMES
Box 99 318 Copper St.
Greenwood, BC, V0H 1J0
Tel: 250-445-2233
Fax: 250-445-2240

HOPE STANDARD
Box 1090 Suite 3, 895 Third Ave.
Hope, BC, V0X 1L0
Tel: 604-869-2421
Fax: 604-869-7351

HOUSTON TODAY
Box 899 3232 Hwy 16 Houston Mall
Houston, BC, V0J 1Z0
Tel: 250-845-2890
Fax: 250-845-7893

INVERMERE VALLEY ECHO
Box 70 530 13th St.
Invermere, BC, V0A 1K0
Tel: 250-342-9216
Fax: 250-342-3930

KAHTOU NEWS
Box 192 5526 Sinku Drive
Sechelt, BC, V0A 3A0
Tel: 1-800-561-4311
Fax: 604-885-7397

KAMLOOPS THIS WEEK
1365 B Dalhousie Drive
Kamloops, BC, V2C 5P6
Tel: 250-374-7467
Fax: 250-374-1033

KELOWNA CAPITAL NEWS
2495 Enterprise Way
Kelowna, BC, V1X 7K2
Tel: 250-763-3212
Fax: 250-763-8469

KITIMAT NORTHERN SENTINEL/ WEEKEND ADVERTISER
626 Enterprise Ave.
Kitimat, BC, V8C 2E4
Tel: 250-632-6144
Fax: 250-639-9373

LADYSMITH CHEMAINUS CHRONICLE
Box 400 341 1st Ave.
Ladysmith, BC, V0R 2E0
Tel: 250-245-2277
Fax: 250-245-2260

LAKE COWICHAN GAZETTE
Box 10 170E Cowichan Lake Road
Lake Cowichan, BC, V0R 2G0
Tel: 250-749-4383
Fax: 250-749-4385

LAKE COWICHAN LAKE NEWS
Box 962 101-205 South Shore Rd.
Lake Cowichan, BC, V0R 2G0
Tel: 250-749-3143
Fax: 250-749-3153

LANGLEY ADVANCE NEWS
111-20353 64 Ave.
Langley, BC, V2Y 1N5
Tel: 604-534-8641
Fax: 604-534-3383

LANGLEY TIMES
Box 3097 20258 Fraser Highway
Langley, BC, V3A 4R3
Tel: 604-533-4157
Fax: 604-533-0219

LANTZVILLE LOG
Box 268 3958 Jacks Road
Lantzville, BC, V0R 2H0
Tel: 250-390-2847
Fax: 250-390-2847

LILLOOET BRIDGE RIVER NEWS
Box 709 979 Main St.
Lillooet, BC, V0K 1V0
Tel: 250-256-4219
Fax: 250-256-4210

MACKENZIE TIMES
540 Mackenzie Blvd.
Mackenzie, BC, V0J 2C0
Tel: 250-997-6675
Fax: 250-997-4747

MAPLE RIDGE PITT MEADOWS NEWS
22328 119th Ave.
Maple Ridge, BC, V2X 2Z3
Tel: 604-467-1122
Fax: 604-463-4741

MAPLE RIDGE PITT MEADOWS TIMES
22334 Selkirk Ave.
Maple Ridge, BC, V2X 2X5
Tel: 604-463-2281
Fax: 604-463-9943

MERRITT HERALD
Box 9 2090 Granite St.
Merritt, BC, V1K 1B8
Tel: 250-378-4241
Fax: 250-378-6818

MERRITT NEWS
Box 939 1950 Quilchena Ave.
Merritt, BC, V1K 1B8
Tel: 250-378-8876
Fax: 250-378-8853

MISSION CITY RECORD
33047 1st Ave.
Mission, BC, V2V 1G2
Tel: 604-826-6221
Fax: 604-826-8266

NAKUSP ARROW LAKES NEWS
Box 189 204 Broadway St
Nakusp, BC, V0G 1R0
Tel: 250-265-3823
Fax: 250-265-3841

NANAIMO BULLETIN
777B Poplar St
Nanaimo, BC, V9S 2H7
Tel: 250-753-3707
Fax: 250-753-0788

NANAIMO HARBOUR CITY STAR
2575 Mccullough Road Suite B1
Nanaimo, BC, V9S 5W5
Tel: 250-729-4200
Fax: 250-729-4256

NELSON KOOTENAY WEEKLY EXPRESS
554 Ward St.
Nelson, BC, V1L 1S9
Tel: 250-354-3910
Fax: 250-352-5075

NELSON PENNYWISE
Box 430 331 Front St.
Kaslo, BC, V0G 1M0
Tel: 1-800-663-4619
Fax: 250-353-7444

NEW WESTMINSTER NEWS LEADER
6569 Kingsway
Burnaby, BC, V5E 1E1
Tel: 604-438-6397
Fax: 604-438-2815

NEW WESTMINSTER RECORD
418 6th St.
New Westminster, BC, V3L 3B2
Tel: 604-525-6306
Fax: 604-525-7360

NICOLA THOMPSON TODAY
Box 9 2090 Granite St.
Merritt, BC, V0K 2B0
Tel: 250-378-4241
Fax: 250-378-6818

OAK BAY NEWS
1824 Store St.
Victoria, BC, V8T 4R4
Tel: 250-598-4123
Fax: 250-386-2624

OLIVER CHRONICLE
Box 880 36083 97th St.
Oliver, BC, V0H 1T0
Tel: 250-498-3711
Fax: 250-498-3966

OSOYOOS TIMES
Box 359 8712 Main St.
Osoyoos, BC, V0H 1V0
Tel: 250-495-7225
Fax: 250-495-6616

PARKSVILLE, THE MORNING SUN
Box 45 114 East Hirst
Parksville, BC, V9P 2G3
Tel: 250-954-0600
Fax: 250-954-0601

PARKSVILLE QUALICUM BEACH NEWS
Box 1180 #4 - 154 Middleton Ave.
Parksville, BC, V9P 2H2
Tel: 250-248-4341
Fax: 250-248-4655

PEACHLAND SIGNAL
Box 800 #3-4478 3rd St.
Peachland, BC, V0H 1X0
Tel: 250-767-2004
Fax: 250-767-3306

PENTICTON WESTERN NEWS
2250 Camrose St.
Penticton, BC, V2A 8R1
Tel: 250-492-0444
Fax: 250-492-9843

PORT HARDY NORTH ISLAND GAZETTE
Box 458 7305 Market St.
Port Hardy, BC, V0N 2P0
Tel: 250-949-6225
Fax: 250-949-7655

POWELL RIVER NEWS
7030 Alberni St.
Powell River, BC, V8A 2C3
Tel: 604-485-4255
Fax: 604-485-5832

POWELL RIVER PEAK
4400 Marine Ave.
Powell River, BC, V8A 2K1
Tel: 604-485-5313
Fax: 604-485-5007

POWELL RIVER TOWN CRIER
7030 Alberni St.
Powell River, BC, V8A 2C3
Tel: 604-485-4255
Fax: 604-485-5832

PRINCE GEORGE FREE PRESS
#200 - 1515 Second Ave
Prince George, BC, V2L 3B8
Tel: 250-564-0005
Fax: 250-562-0025

PRINCE GEORGE THIS WEEK
145 Brunswick St.
Prince George, BC, V2L 2B2
Tel: 250-563-9988
Fax: 250-562-5012

PRINCETON, THE SIMILKAMEEN SPOTLIGHT
Box 340 298 Bridge St.
Princeton, BC, V0X 1W0
Tel: 250-295-3535
Fax: 250-295-7322

QUEEN CHARLOTTE ISLANDS OBSERVER
Box 205 623 7th St.
Queen Charlotte, BC, V0T 1S0
Tel: 250-559-4680
Fax: 250-559-8433

QUESNEL CARIBOO OBSERVER
188 Carson Ave.
Quesnel, BC, V2J 2A8
Tel: 250-992-2121
Fax: 250-992-5229

REVELSTOKE TIMES-REVIEW
Box 20 402 Third St. West
Revelstoke, BC, V0E 2S0
Tel: 250-837-4667
Fax: 250-837-2003

RICHMOND NEWS
5731 No. 3 Road
Richmond, BC, V6X 2C9
Tel: 604-270-8031
Fax: 604-270-2248

RICHMOND REVIEW
140-5671 #3 Road
Richmond, BC, V6X 2C7
Tel: 604-606-8700
Fax: 604-606-8752

SAANICH NEWS
1824 Store St.
Victoria, BC, V8T 4R4
Tel: 250-920-2090
Fax: 250-920-7352

**SALMON ARM OBSERVER/
SHUSWAP MARKET**
Box 550 51 Hudson St.
Salmon Arm, BC, V1E 4N7
Tel: 250-832-2131
Fax: 250-832-5140

SECHELT EXPRESS
C/O Gibsons Coast Independent
Box 125 #4-292 Gower Point Road
Gibsons, BC, V0N 1V0
Tel: 604-886-4003
Fax: 604-886-4993

**SECHELT/ GIBSONS COAST
INDEPENDENT**
Box 125 #4-292 Gower Point Road
Gibsons, BC, V0N 1V0
Tel: 604-886-4003
Fax: 604-886-4993

**SECHELT SUNSHINE COAST
REPORTER**
Box 1388 5683 Cowrie St.
Sechelt, BC, V0N 3A0
Tel: 604-885-4811
Fax: 604-885-4818

SALMON ARM, SHUSWAP SUN
Box 729 121D Shuswap St. N.W.
Salmon Arm, BC, V1E 4N8
Tel: 250-832-6364
Fax: 250-832-2206

SICAMOUS EAGLE VALLEY NEWS
Box 113 1133 Parksville St.
Sicamous, BC, V0E 2V0
Tel: 250-836-2570
Fax: 250-836-2661

**SIDNEY PENINSULA NEWS
REVIEW**
Box 2070 9726 First St.
Sidney, BC, V8L 3C9
Tel: 250-656-1151
Fax: 250-656-5526

SMITHERS INTERIOR NEWS
Box 2560 3764 Broadway Ave.
Smithers, BC, V0J 2N0
Tel: 250-847-3266
Fax: 250-847-2995

SOOKE NEWS MIRROR
Box 339 6711 Eustace Road
Sooke, BC, V0S 1N0
Tel: 250-642-5752
Fax: 250-642-4767

**OKANAGAN FALLS, SOUTH
OKANAGAN REVIEW**
Box 220 10 - 1133 Main St.
Okanagan Falls, BC, V0H 1R0
Tel: 250-497-8880
Fax: 250-497-8860

**SPARWOOD, THE ELK VALLEY
MINER**
Box 820 Greenwood Mall Annex 110
Centennial Square
Sparwood, BC, V0B 2G0
Tel: 250-425-6411
Fax: 250-423-4222

SQUAMISH CHIEF
Box 3500 38113 2nd Ave.
Squamish, BC, V0N 3G0
Tel: 604-892-9161
Fax: 604-892-8483

SUMMERLAND REVIEW
Box 309 13226 North Victoria Road
Summerland, BC, V0H 1Z0
Tel: 250-494-5406
Fax: 250-494-5453

SURREY NORTH DELTA LEADER
Box 276Suite 103 9180 King George
Hwy
Surrey, BC, V5E 7H5
Tel: 604-588-4313
Fax: 604-588-2246

SURREY, NORTH DELTA, WHITE ROCK, THE NOW
201 - 7889 132 Ave.
Surrey, BC, V3W 4N2
Tel: 604-572-0064
Fax: 604-572-6438

TERRACE STANDARD
3210 Clinton St.
Terrace, BC, V8G 5R2
Tel: 250-638-7283
Fax: 250-638-8432

TOFINO UCLUELET WESTERLY NEWS
Box 317 1701 Peninsula Road
Ucluelet, BC, V0R 3A0
Tel: 250-726-7029
Fax: 250-732-3961

TUMBLER RIDGE OBSERVER
901 -100th Ave.
Dawson Creek, BC, V1G 1W2
Tel: 250-782-4888
Fax: 250-732-3961

VALEMOUNT MCBRIDE, THE VALLEY SENTINEL
Box 688 1012 Commercial Drive
Valemount, BC, V0E 2Z0
Tel: 250-566-4425
Fax: 250-566-4528

VANCOUVER COURIER
1574 W. 6th Ave.
Vancouver, BC, V6J 1R2
Tel: 604-738-1411
Fax: 604-731-1474

VANCOUVER ECHO
3355 Grandview Highway
Vancouver, BC, V5M 1Z5
Tel: 604-437-7030
Fax: 604-439-3367

NORTH VANCOUVER, THE NORTH SHORE NEWS
1139 Lonsdale Ave.
North Vancouver, BC, V7M 2H4
Tel: 604-985-2131
Fax: 604-985-3227

VANCOUVER WEST END TIMES
522-510 W.Hastings St.
Vancouver, BC, V6B 1L8
Tel: 604-682-1424
Fax: 604-682-1425

VANCOUVER WEST ENDER
Suite 103 2145 West Broadway
Vancouver, BC, V6K 4L3
Tel: 604-606-8677
Fax: 604-606-8687

VANDERHOOF OMINECA EXPRESS
Box 1007 150 West Columbia St.
Vanderhoof, BC, V0J 3A0
Tel: 250-567-9258
Fax: 250-567-2070

VERNON, THE MORNING STAR
4407 - 25th Ave.
Vernon, BC, V1T 1P5
Tel: 250-545-3322
Fax: 250-542-1510

VERNON SUN
3309 - 31st Ave
Vernon, BC,
V1T 2H4
Tel: 250-549-1191
Fax: 250-549-4446

VICTORIA MONDAY MAGAZINE
1609 Blanshard St.
Victoria, BC, V8W 2J5
Tel: 250-382-6188
Fax: 250-381-2662

VICTORIA NEWS
1824 Store St.
Victoria, BC, V8T 4R4
Tel: 250-381-3484
Fax: 250-386-2624

**WESTBANK, THE WESTSIDE
WEEKLY**
140-2300 Carrington Road
Westbank, BC V4T 2E6
Tel: 250-768-5030
Fax: 250-768-4276

WHISTLER QUESTION
#238 - 4370 Lorimer Road
Whistler, BC, V0N 1B4
Tel: 604-932-5131
Fax: 604-932-2862

**WHITE ROCK, THE PEACE ARCH
NEWS**
Box 75149
(101-1440 George St.)
Surrey, BC, V4A 9M4
Tel: 604-531-1711
Fax: 604-531-7977

WHITEHORSE YUKON NEWS
211 Wood St.
Whitehorse, Yukon, Y1A 2E4
Tel: 1-867-667-6285
Fax: 1-867-668-3755

**WILLIAMS LAKE TRIBUNE/
WEEKENDER**
188 N. 1st Ave.
Williams Lake, BC, V2G 1Y8
Tel: 250-392-2331
Fax: 250-392-7253

WINFIELD CALENDAR
#1-10058 Highway 97
Winfield, BC, V4V 1P8
Tel: 250-766-4688
Fax: 250-766-4645

BCYCNA PRESIDENTS SINCE FORMATION IN 1922.

1922 — Loius F. Ball, Vernon News, Vernon, B.C.
1923-24 — Hugh Savage, Cowichan Leader, Duncan, B.C.
1925 — J.A. Bates, Semiahmoo Sun, White Rock,B.C.
1926-27 — Ralph E. White, Kamloops Sentinel, Kamloops, B.C.
1928 — Ben Hughes Comox, Argus, Courtenay, B.C.
1929 – Jack H. Mohr Revelstoke, Review, Revelstoke, B.C.
1930 — W.A. Elletson, Rossland Miner, Rossland, B.C.
1931 — Charles A. Barber, Chilliwack Progress, Chilliwack, B.C.
1932-33 — William S. Harris, Vernon News, Vernon, B.C.
1934 — Thomas A. Love, Grand Forks Gazette, Grand Forks, B.C.
1935-36 — Ernest B. Mayon, Merritt Herald, Merritt, B.C.
1937 — G.W.A. Smith, Surrey Leader, Cloverdale, B.C.
1938 — Robert J. McDougall, Penticton Herald, Penticton, B.C.
1939-40 — J.B. Creighton, Cowichan Leader, Duncan, B.C.
1941 — Edgar Dunning, Ladner Optimist, Ladner, B.C.
1942 — Don Campbell, The Observer, Salmon Arm, B.C.
1943 — Hugh McIntyre, Sidney Review, Sidney, B.C.
1944 — Lang Sands, Fraser Valley Record, Mission, B.C.
1945 — Les Way, Powell River News, Powell River, B.C.
1946 — Grev Rowland, Penticton Herald, Penticton, B.C.
1947 — Roy P. McLean, Kelowna Courier, Kelowna, B.C.
1948 — Irving Wilson, West Coast Advocate, Port Alberni, B.C.
1949 — Frank R. Harris, Vernon News, Vernon, B.C.
1950 — Al Alsgard, Powell River News, Powell River, B.C.
1951 — Stanley Orris, Grand Forks Gazette, Grand Forks, B.C.
1952 — Victor Ball, Fernie Free Press, Fernie, B.C.
1953 — Lew Griffiths, Cariboo Observer, Quesnel, B.C.
1954 — Ronald White, Kamloops Sentinel, Kamloops, B.C.
1955 — Leslie E. Barber, Chilliwack Progress, Chilliwack, B.C.
1956 — James E. Jamieson, Armstrong Advertiser, Armstrong, B.C.
1957 — John McNaughton, Ladysmith Chronicle, Ladysmith, B.C.
1958 — Eric. Dunning, Haney Gazette, Haney, B.C.
1959 – Arvid W. Lundell, Revelstoke Review, Revelstoke, B.C.
1960 — Cecil Hacker, Abbotsford News, Abbotsford, B.C.
1961 — Les Campbell, Castlegar News, Castlegar, B.C.
1962 — Clive Stangoe, Williams Lake Tribune, Williams Lake, B.C.
1963 — Will Dobson, Cowichan Leader, Duncan, B.C.
1964 — Fred Cruice, Sunshine Coast News, Gibsons, B.C.
1965 — Nestor Izowsky, White Rock Sun, White Rock, B.C.
1966 — Don Somerville, Oliver Chronicle, Oliver, B.C.
1967 — Dan Murray, Alaska Highway News, Fort St. John, B.C.
1968 — Cliff Hacker, Abbotsford News, Abbotsford, B.C.

1969 — Herb Legg, Creston Review, Creston, B.C.
1970 — Cloudesley Hoodspith, Lions Gate Times, West Vancouver, B.C.
1971 — Jim Schatz, Langley Advance, Langley, B.C.
1972 — Stan Stodola, Osoyoos Times, Osoyoos, B.C.
1973 — Alan Black, Williams Lake Tribune, B.C.
1974 — Gordon Root, White Rock, B.C.
1975 — Fred Traff, 100 Mile House Free Press, B.C.
1976 — Ernie Bexley, Delta Optimist, Delta, B.C.
1977-78 — Frank Richards, Gulf Islands Driftwood, Salt Spring Island, B.C.
1979 — Dave Gamble, Summerland Review, Summerland, B.C.
1980 — Denis Stanley, Arrow Lakes News, Nakusp, B.C.
1981 — Rose Tatlow , Squamish Chief, B.C.
1982 — David Black, Black Press, Victoria, B.C.
1983 — Rollie Rose, Ladysmith-Chemainus Chronicle, B.C.
1984 — Ian Wickett, Salmon Arm Observer, B.C.
1985 — Ross Mavis, North Island Gazette, Port Hardy, B.C.
1986 — Peter Speck, North Shore News, North Vancouver, B.C.
1987 — Tony Richards, Gulf Islands Driftwood, Salt Spring Island, B.C.
1988 — Jeff den Biesen, Lillooet News, Lillooet, B.C.
1989 — Luke Vorstermans, 100 Mile House Free Press, 100 Mile House, B.C.
1990 — Joyce Carlson, Powell River Peak, Powell River, B.C.
1991 — Bob Grainger, Williams Lake Tribune, Williams Lake, B.C.
1992 — Tom Siba, Delta Optimist, Delta, B.C.
1993 — Andrew Lynch, Victoria Monday Magazine, Victoria, B.C.
1994 — Manfred Templemayr, Duncan Cowichan News Leader, Duncan, B.C.
1995 — Richard Odo, Parksville-Qualicum Beach Morning Sun, B.C.
1995-97 — Steve Houston, Lower Mainland Publishing Ltd., Vancouver, B.C.
1997-99 — Penny Graham, Squamish Chief, Squamish, B.C.

ABOUT THE EDITOR/AUTHOR

George Affleck has spent the last ten years working as a writer and broadcaster. He has lived and worked around the world—Denmark, Sweden, England, Israel, Egypt, Greece and Taiwan. Working on *Paper Trails: A History of BC and Yukon Community Newspapers* gave George the chance to learn more about the part of the world he was born and raised in. This is George's first book. He is currently completing his second, a walking guide to Vancouver City.